FAIR WARNING

Why Real Societal Solutions Begin at Home

Revised and Updated

by Jeff Chavez

KIBERA PRESS

555 W. 5th Street
35th Floor
Los Angeles, CA 90013

Second Edition, 2020

Book Cover Design by James Wetz

Manufactured in the United States of America
10 9 8 7 6 5 4 3 2 1

ISBN 978-1-09832-853-5

Dedicated to my wife and kids

Family Portrait by Brenna Chavez, 16 years old
The Chavez Family (from left to right)—Luke Jeffrey Chavez (21), Darcy Chavez King (23),
Bradley King, Allison Chavez Terry (25), Marigold Terry (7mo), Austin Terry, Jeff and
Leesa Chavez, Braden Chavez (18), Brenna Chavez (16), Megan Chavez (13), and Bryce
Chavez (11)

Contents

Children Learn What They Live

If a child lives with criticism, he learns to condemn.
If a child lives with hostility, he learns to fight.
If a child lives with fear, he learns to be apprehensive.
If a child lives with pity, he learns to feel sorry for himself.
If a child lives with jealousy, he learns to hate.
If a child lives with encouragement, he learns to be confident.
If a child lives with tolerance, he learns to be patient.
If a child lives with praise, he learns to be appreciative.
If a child lives with acceptance, he learns to love.
If a child lives with approval, he learns to like himself.
If a child lives with recognition, he learns to have a goal.
If a child lives with fairness, he learns justice.
If a child lives with security, he learns to have faith in himself
and those around him.
If a child lives with honesty, he learns what truth is.
If a child lives with friendliness, he learns that the
world is a nice place in which to live.
—Dorthy L. Nolte

Twenty-Three Years Later

I t's July 23, 2020. America strains under a months-long Covid-19 quarantine. As a result, the country finds itself in an economic tailspin. More than 20 million Americans are out of work. Simultaneously, social tension, political back-stabbing, and chaos have reached a fever-pitch in the aftermath of George Floyd's death. Minneapolis police officer, Derek Chauvin, and four other officers, now face murder charges for this horrific killing that was witnessed by the world. Fear, uncertainty, civil unrest, racial division, and rising crime dominate our headlines every day. Our economic, democratic, and social fabric now hangs by a thread.

All our high hopes for 2020 came to a screeching halt in March of this year. No American, no world citizen for that matter, has been unaffected. With my business projects now in neutral, I've found myself with unexpected time on my hands. Considering society's current state, I've been revisiting my collection of books on history for insight. Skimming the titles, I found that tucked neatly between them was my book, *Fair Warning*, which I had authored twenty-three years ago. I hadn't picked it up in ages. It felt almost unfamiliar as I laid eyes on it again and thumbed through its pages. Had I really written this little book so long ago?

I fixed on the subtitles, *Making Good Children Great and Turning Ordinary Parents Into American Heroes. A Parenting Perspective from Generation X.* During the '90s, there was a lot of commentary about my generation, *Generation X*—claiming we were lazy, difficult, disinterested, and likely on the road to nowhere special. Similar things were said about us as is being said about *Millennials* today. Perhaps the book was born because I took offense to the stereotypes. In my early 20s, I was already married with two daughters, working hard to build a business. If Gen X was just a bunch of slugs, what about the many peers I knew of who were productive and contributing? I wanted to understand better the difference between the "lazy, difficult, and disinterested," and the ones who would go on to do great things. Into a sociological research wormhole, I went, emerging nearly four years later, with my conclusion, captured in my unexpected little manifesto, *Fair Warning*.

In the book's introduction, I said that the gap between the Gen X stereotype and becoming someone great came down to this: *The difference is in the home. There is a direct and undeniable correlation between what's taught in the home and young people's ability to begin making the choices that will lead them to inevitable sorrow or unparalleled joy. Many young people fall into the traps of premature sexuality, drugs, violence, racism, and laziness because they're left to their own devices, void of wisdom, and without consistent love and direction from parents. In many cases, these experiences prove to haunt their lives for many years, even a lifetime.* From this point of reference, I attempted to make the case that parents can do more than the government or institutions to improve society.

Having re-read *Fair Warning* in 2020, I find my convictions about its message are more resolute than when I wrote it. Surprisingly, it's more relevant now than it was then.

Here's why: First, any half-attentive observer can see that our society is suffering through a crisis of character that is more severe than any time in recent memory. Second, from a factual and statistical standpoint, our social problems have continued to increase in the last twenty-three years since the book was written. Finally, observation and statistics reveal the undeniable correlation between detrimental social behavior and the breakdown of family leadership. Because of these realities, America now strains under the collective consequences of racism, drug and alcohol abuse, political corruption, sexual assault, dysfunctional homes, crime, incarceration, materialism, negativity, declining spirituality, and a myriad of crippling addictions.

Consider just a handful of these current findings selected from more than 20 pages of similar data:

- An analysis of 50 separate studies of juvenile crime revealed that the prevalence of delinquency in broken homes was 10–15% higher than in intact homes. Also, there were no appreciable differences in the impact of broken homes between girls and boys or between black youths and white youth *(Edward Wells and Joseph Rankin, "Families and Delinquency: A Meta-Analysis of the Impact of Broken Homes," Social Problems 38: 71–89).*

- A study of adolescents convicted of homicide in adult court found that at the time of the crimes, 42.9% of their parents had never been married, 29.5% were divorced, and 8.9% were separated. Less than 20% of these children were from married parent households *(Patrick Darby, Wesley Allan, Javad Kashani, Kenneth Hartke and John Reid, "Analysis of 112 Juveniles Who Committed Homicide: Characteristics and a Closer Look at Family Abuse," Journal of Family Violence: 365–374).*

- Boys who are fatherless from birth are 3.061 times as likely to go to jail as peers from intact families, while boys who do not see their father depart until they are 10 to 14 years old are 2.396 times as likely to go to jail as peers from intact families *(Cynthia C. Harper and Sara S. McLanahan, "Father Absence and Youth Incarceration," Journal of Research on Adolescence: 369–397).*

- 1.3 women (age 18 and over) in the United States are forcibly raped each minute. That translates to 78 an hour, 1,871 per day, or 683,000 per year *(Rape in America: A Report to the Nation, Arlington, VA: National Victim Center)*

- 13.3% of college women indicated that they had been forced to have sex in a dating situation *(Johnson, I, Sigler R, "Forced Sexual Intercourse Among Intimates," Journal of Interpersonal Violence.)*

- Between 1/3 and 2/3 of known sexual assault victims are age 15 or younger *(Population Information Program. Population Reports: Ending Violence Against Women. Johns Hopkins School of Public Health and Center for Healthcare Gender Equity.)*

- Sexual violence on campus is pervasive. Among undergraduate students, 23.1% of females and 5.4% of males experience rape or sexual assault through physical force, violence, or incapacitation *(David Cantor, Bonnie Fisher, Susan Chibnall, Reanna Townsend, et al. Association of American Universities (AAU), Report on the AAU Campus Climate Survey on Sexual Assault and Sexual Misconduct).*

- In 2018, 26.5% of people 18 or older reported that they engaged in binge drinking in the past month *(National Institute on Alcohol Abuse and Alcoholism).*

- According to the 2018 NSDUH, 14.4 million adults ages 18 and older had Alcohol Use Disorder (AUD). An estimated 400,000 adolescents ages 12–17 had AUD *(National Institute on Alcohol Abuse and Alcoholism).*

- More than 10% of US children live with a parent with alcohol problems, while alcohol misuse costs the United States over $375 billion *(National Institute on Alcohol Abuse and Alcoholism).*

- Opioids were involved in 46,802 overdose deaths in 2018 (69.5% of all drug overdose deaths). Two out of three (67.0%) opioid-involved overdose deaths include synthetic opioids *(Centers for Disease Control and Prevention).*

- Among married two-parent families, whether white or black, the crime rate was very low. The capacity and determination to maintain stable married relationships, not race, was cited as the pivotal factor. Chaotic, broken communities resulted from chaotic, broken families *(Patrick Fagan, "The Real Root Causes of Violent Crime: The Breakdown of Marriage, Family, and Community," The Heritage Foundation, Backgrounder #1026).*

- In 2018 and 2019, 65% of American adults describe themselves as Christians when asked about their religion, down 12 percentage points over the past decade.

Meanwhile, the religiously unaffiliated share of the population, consisting of people who describe their religious identity as atheist, agnostic or "nothing" now stands at 26%, up from 17% in 2009 *(Pew Research Center, "In US, Decline of Christianity Continues at Rapid Pace: An Update on America's Changing Religious Landscape," Oct. 17, 2019).*

We can discuss, debate, and analyze cultural statistics every which way. But at the end of the day, we can't deny that we are living through a massive social crisis. In raw numbers, we're talking about more than 50 million of our friends and neighbors who, at this very moment, are directly impacted by any combination of addiction, crime, racism, injustice, abuse, manipulation, or emotional distress. Worldwide, it's billions.

Revisiting *Fair Warning* was very difficult for me. Like reading an old journal, at times, I winced with embarrassment and shame. When I wrote the book, I thought I understood my topic well. Conceptually, I did. But it was impossible to understand then how challenging life would become. I had not yet fully practiced these concepts myself. At the time, I would've laughed if you'd have told me that I would suffer through some of the very character failures of which I was passionately warning readers. Yet, that is precisely the case.

Not long after the publication of *Fair Warning*, ironically, my life began to unwind. Through a combination of carelessness, arrogance, and pride, I developed some bad habits that I kept tucked neatly away from discovery. Over time, just as I had explained in my own book, those habits became addictions, and I found myself caught in a web too powerful to escape without help. Like so many before me, I tried in vain to manage the situation alone, only compounding the problems. Ultimately, I was met with severe consequences. And worse, the undeserved consequences suffered by those I claimed to love the most, were crushing. At the age of 34, I lost everything. My wife divorced me. Our three children endured what was a shattered world in their young lives because of me. The company I had founded and operated as CEO crumbled, and my reputation was ruined. I found myself alone in a small apartment, broken-hearted, unable to tuck my kids into bed every night, disgraced, ashamed, spiritually depleted, clinically depressed, and more than $2 million in debt. There was nobody to blame but myself. I stared blankly into an uphill battle that would require more than a decade of recovery, restitution, faith, and healing.

The choice before me was simple. I could get up, dust off, move forward, or slump away and out of sight. I chose to get up and keep trying. Over time and with a massive amount of persistence and hope, I began to recover and heal. I began to change. Relationships began to mend. Gratefully, my relationship with my children survived and has thrived. We learned from the profound lessons together. Eventually, I was re-married to a wonderful, talented woman and have welcomed her four young children as my own. My professional pursuits have rebounded. And my spiritual life is in order. Today, my life is full and vibrant again, and I thank God for that. But from now on, day-by-day, my attention to the principles of honesty, integrity, and humility is my highest priority. Because I know first-hand how hard and far we can fall.

And this is where my 2020 re-reading of *Fair Warning* was a powerful personal awakening for me. Yes, at first, I felt that sting of hypocrisy and embarrassment for failing to hold firm to the things I had written and advised about. But as I continued to read, I was moved to tears by the fact that my failures notwithstanding, I had, ultimately, held firm. Regarding our shortcomings, especially when we know what is right and do wrong anyway, I had written these words in the 2nd Chapter, "The Most Powerful Position in America": "When they make mistakes, they're able to learn from them and begin to change. If bad habits are sown, they know there is no habit or weakness too great to overcome. They know that drug use can be curbed. Stealing, lying, and cheating are character flaws that can be overcome with determination."

Only now have I learned for myself what the most important message from this little book is. It is this: **We *must* do the** *best that we can. We will make mistakes along the way. But we must never give up!*

I never gave up. I never abandoned my pursuit of developing principles that I knew in my heart of hearts would bring the most joy, safety, and prosperity. As a child, it was my parents who taught me those things. They gave me *Fair Warning* about life's dangers and pitfalls, and that we get back up when we stumble. And though I have failed during many of life's seasons, I knew that I must keep getting back up to become better. And this, it turns out, is the key to Becoming. As a father to seven, it's now my privilege, along with my wife, to teach these lessons to each of them. It's my responsibility, our responsibility, to give them a *Fair Warning* about life's dangers and pitfalls as my parents did for me.

Now, more than ever, I believe that the most important work we can do in life is to raise generations of great men and women. Our current social crisis goes much deeper than what appears to be a matter of political parties or policies on the surface. What we are witnessing is a crisis of character. It is a crisis born from a lack of leadership by parents for their children. If we want real change, this must change.

What follows here are the original Preface, Introduction, and Chapters of *Fair Warning* written in 1997, with only minor grammatical and structural edits.

As you dive into this book, you'll likely recognize that it has aged a bit, and the writing certainly isn't award-winning. That being said, I hope you'll find the message more relevant now than it was then. My heartfelt plea is that you will resolve to make an unwavering commitment to lead powerfully in your home. Indeed, a resolve that will become your life's legacy and your most significant contribution to society.

Preface

I'm a *Generation Xer* (born between 1961 and 1981). I've grown up as a teen of the '80s and 90s. There is nothing reported about today's youth that I've not been personally affected by.

I believe my life hung in the balance as a teen toward eventual success or toward a lifetime of failures and avoidable difficulties. Opportunities to do wrong seemed to engulf me constantly. I was pressured to sneak into a friend's alcohol cabinet while his parents were away for the weekend when I was in the 4th grade. During the summer of that same year, my friend showed me his dad's two-and-a-half-foot stack of *Playboy* magazines, which sat in the living room bookcase. In the 6th grade, my grandmother's 14-year-old neighbor invited me to his bedroom to watch him smoke marijuana while his parents watched *The Joker's Wild* in the next room. Between the 7th and 9th grades, I was offered cocaine, ecstasy, and LSD. Then I watched as one of my closest friends strung himself out on cocaine and dropped out of school for a year and a half. By the time I was 16 years old, nearly all of my male friends, except for myself and a few others, had lost their virginity. All around me was cheating, theft, and vandalism among schoolmates as early as elementary school. These activities increased as I went through my high school years. I watched violent gang fights at our campus every month. During my senior year, a member of my wrestling team was shot and killed in a drive-by shooting. One of the first girls I ever had a crush on, committed suicide the night of our senior prom.

These things took place in a lovely, suburban community in Southern California. I shudder to think of the stories inner-city youth can tell.

Now in 1997, at 26 years old, I'm the father of two beautiful daughters. Thankfully, my life has both purpose and direction. As a young man, I chose to walk away from the pitfalls that many in my generation fall into. Why? Why did I escape the trappings when so many others did not? What makes the difference?

The difference is in the home. There is a direct and undeniable correlation between what's taught in the home and young people's ability to begin making the choices that will lead them to inevitable sorrow or unparalleled joy. Many young people fall into the traps of premature sexuality, drugs, violence, racism, and laziness because they're left to their own devices, void of wisdom, and without consistent love and direction from parents. In many cases, these experiences prove to haunt their lives for many years, even a lifetime.

Somewhere along the way, I began to recognize the wisdom of the *Fair Warnings,* which my parents placed before me. I crossed the bridge linking my parents' rules and guidelines to my own standards. I was beginning to find congruence with the wisdom of my parents.

This occurred as I began to face the realities of life. I knew I needed and wanted to make wise decisions. Where would I go? What would I do for a career? How would I support a family? How would I achieve my goals? I found these questions, and their answers were far more significant than those of the years of trivial teen decisions. Now I could see I had serious choices to make concerning my life. Now I could see that life is a continual process of correcting our mistakes and gradually improving ourselves. I now owned the teachings of my parents, learned at a very early age.

There are countless unheralded Generation Xers and other individuals who have made that same resolve. And despite the constant, day-to-day difficulties of life, they're achieving great things and are living beautiful lives. But there are many more who are not. They have not yet claimed their roles as true men or women but continue to linger in the now and squander their potential on the lesser, temporary pleasures of life. They find themselves in a state of disappointment and difficulty as lasting gratification escapes them.

Many of these teen-minded individuals are not just *Generation Xers*. Many of them are 40, 50, and 60 years old. Some of them are drug addicts on the street. Some of them are executives in major corporations. Some are your average, unassuming neighbors who defer their opportunity to raise exceptional children. They do this by allowing the media, schools, and peers to shape their children's lives and become their most significant influence. These people are simultaneously unaware or simply not concerned that their most significant opportunities for real joy and satisfaction in life are swiftly passing by them.

Because of this, I decided to try and deliver a message, which would hit home and affect a wide range of readers. I spent over three years researching and compiling data on the family and society. I reviewed, outlined, and organized the crucial lessons I learned from my parents and my own experiences. I pondered over the perspectives and backgrounds of the many teens that I've had the opportunity to teach about living lives of principle. These experiences and thoughts about them were initially recorded on over 1,000 pages of journal entries throughout my childhood and young adult years. *Fair Warning* is the result of this effort.

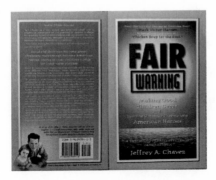

(Original Book Cover of First Edition, 1997)

Introduction

FAIR WARNING: Parents' commitment to teach and forewarn their children about the many dangers of life. Parents' commitment to teach their children the virtues of honesty, hard work, humility, self-discipline, and service.

All children need and deserve *Fair Warnings* about what threatens them and about what protects them. However, often, they don't receive them. I'm talking about head-on, crystal-clear lessons on how and why to avoid negative attitudes, dishonesty, drugs, violence, and promiscuity. Powerful lessons about how and why to develop the principles of kindness, honesty, frugality, self-mastery, and spirituality. These are some of the *Fair Warnings* that will carry them through their teen years and provide them with the ability to remain devoted to correct principles throughout their lives.

When parents neglect these *Fair Warnings*, the odds of rearing truly successful children radically diminish. The odds of raising children who continually make poor decisions in life significantly increases.

I recall the story of Roy Reigels, who, after recovering a fumble in the 1929 Rose Bowl and in a state of disorientation, ran the length of the field toward the end zone. Reveling in the crowd's wild roars of excitement and unusually loud cheering, Roy was violently tackled at the 1-yard line by his teammate. Roy was about to score for the opposing team! Being tackled was a valuable course correction for Roy's side, no doubt. Yes, they had lost a lot of ground, but they still had a chance to start moving in the right direction again.

As we neglect to teach truth and provide *Fair Warnings* to our children, we're not unlike Roy Reigels, who seemed to be experiencing the glory of his progress, only to be sorely disappointed when he realized his misguided efforts.

I remember when I dreaded taking my car to the shop because of the awful noises, which bellowed from under the hood. I was convinced that I couldn't afford the needed repairs. Much to my surprise, after finally giving in to the howling within my hood, the mechanic reached deep within the engine and re-attached a disconnected valve. The cost? Only $20.00. This simple procedure eliminated the awful noises and relieved me of my haunting financial concerns.

Indeed, there are serious mechanical problems that occur despite our efforts to maintain our vehicles. But many costly repairs can be minimized or avoided through regular, proper maintenance.

We learn that small, consistent course corrections or maintenance will influence our children's ability to choose a better course. Thoughtful course corrections will serve to motivate our youth to expect more of themselves. They'll develop a desire to go forward as bridled, productive achievers rather than haphazard, aimless coasters.

I hope that my views and experiences will motivate readers to re-evaluate and deeply contemplate the critical role we have as builders of a great society. I hope to stir readers with factual information about these *Fair Warnings*, information about which most adults have long been aware of but may have overlooked in the rush of life. I hope that readers will come away from this book with a desire to dedicate themselves to being the best version of themselves.

This book is intended to serve as a starting point for readers to seek more education, information, and instruction about personal change and spirituality from good authors, teachers, parents, and leaders.

Gordon B. Hinkley had said, "What societies need, above all else, is a strengthening of the homes of the people. Every child is a product of a home. Societies are having terrible youth problems, but I am convinced that they have a greater parent problem..." He continued, "What can be done? We cannot affect a turnaround in a day or a month or a year. But I am satisfied that with enough effort, we can begin a turnaround within a generation and accomplish wonders within two generations. That is not a very long time in the history of man. There is nothing any of us can do that will have a greater long-term benefit than to rekindle wherever possible; the kind of spirit within homes in which goodness can flourish."

We will experience true happiness and satisfaction in our lives as we watch our families realize joy and contentment rather than mere temporary pleasures. Most of us possess a natural desire to make a positive and lasting impact on the lives of those we love so dearly, our families. Let's act on those desires. As parents, we are best able to warn our children about all that we know to be destructive. If we do this, not only will we make our own ...*Good Children Great,* we will also become ...*American Heroes.*

SECTION ONE:
The State of the Union

CHAPTER 1:
Pit-Bulls and
American Society

Historically, we see that a nation can survive a multiplicity of disasters, war, invasion, and disease, but no nation has ever been able to survive the disintegration of the family and the home.
—Lucille Johnson

July 18th, 1997. It was a picture-perfect day in Laguna Beach, CA, only 11 days before my 26th birthday. Never in my wildest dreams would I have imagined I would be assaulted by a deadly Pit-bull and a demented Generation Xer that day.

I was relaxing. Taking a break from the appointments of the day and taking advantage of one of my favorite locations. I sat on a bench overlooking the world-renowned Laguna Beach cove. That day, hundreds of tourists and beach-goers were swarming about the beach, swimming in the surf, strolling along the boardwalk, eating lunch on the grass, and watching the heated volleyball and basketball games. I had an hour to spare and was taking it all in and had settled down with a good book.

Suddenly, my thoughts were interrupted by loud and ferocious barking. A Pit-bull was attacking a Siberian husky on a leash walking along with its master. I watched as the two dog owners struggled to separate the animals. The owner of the Pit-bull delivered several rapid blows to the head of his *beloved* pet while yelling at the top of his lungs. Luckily, the two men could separate them before the Pit-bull had a chance to sink its teeth beyond the husky's dense coat.

I was annoyed that this dog-owner wasn't using enough common sense to have such an aggressive and overwhelmingly powerful animal on a leash. I soon discovered my annoyance increasing as I continued to watch the master beat his dog profusely to scold the dog. When the beating ended, he hugged the dog, and kissed it directly on the mouth and, to my utter amazement, released the dog and again allowed it to sniff and wander about unleashed. The owner seemed oblivious to the many small children, hundreds of adults, and other animals.

The young man who owned the dog appeared to be about 21 years old. He wore long shorts hanging so loosely that they rested four or five inches below his waistline. His shorts were sagging because of the long silver chain which hung zoot-suit style from his back pocket to his front pocket. His bare torso revealed his sophisticated art collection, and his head was shaved nearly bald. Indeed, the dog was an asset to his overall image, and to leash the animal probably wasn't the coolest thing to do.

While I was thinking about the absurdity of it all, the Pitbull identified its next target and bolted across the grass toward a small white puppy. The owner chased the animal as fast as he could, screaming for his dog to come back. No chance.

Luckily for the puppy, the Pit-bull over-shot his target as he rapidly came upon the unsuspecting victim. The Pit-bull was so excited and had moved so quickly that it ran right into the little dog, running it over and had to double back to get a hold of it. That gave the Pit-bull's owner the split second he needed to dive across the grass and tackle his dog before it had a chance to attack successfully.

Another beating ensued, and I was yet amazed that there was still no attempt to leash the dog and no effort to consider the safety of those around him.

I was now standing and watching as were many others. Being the type to speak up, I cautiously walked near the owner. When I was within ear-shot, I said directly, but politely, "You know, a dog like that really ought to be on a leash in such a busy place. Somebody's bound to get hurt."

He had his back to me and was bent over, continuing to punish his large and muscular dog. He made no immediate response. He didn't even look my way. I was just about to move on when he quickly snatched up his dog under his right arm, turned and lunged toward me. With a wild look in his eye and a terrible scowl on his face, he yelled, "What did you say?! Do you want some of this dog, punk?"

I backed away as fast as I could, stumbling as I had been caught off-guard. I found myself within inches of the snarling dog (this happens to be one of the few domestic animals that strikes genuine fear in my heart) and answered calmly, "No, actually, I don't want any of your dog. I only asked that you put that animal on a leash."

He continued to rush toward me, yelling and screaming. He told me that he would let his dog loose on me, "How'd you like that...?" he asked sarcastically. He then explained that his dog would break my arm and tear up my leg. All of which I am sure he would have done. He taunted me and repeated again, "Come on, punk, let's fight right now! I'll kill you!"

My heart pounded, and I felt dizzy by the sudden rush of adrenaline. I felt as though I had nowhere to go. I couldn't run, surely the dog would catch me. I couldn't fight back for fear that the dog would get hold of my arms and tear them to shreds. The owner wouldn't listen to reason, and he was relentless. I felt as though I were in a dream. Over 100 people had stopped, just watching and not saying a word. All that I could do was back away as fast as possible. I continued to back up in a continual stumble. I held my hand up in front of me, walking backward in a circle. I was repeating as loud as possible in between his threats and swearing, "Just get that dog away from me! Get that dog out of my face!" To eliminate the possibility of being bitten, I suggested, "Why don't you put the dog away and handle me yourself?" I had no fear of the coward who hid behind his animal compared to the look in that dog's eyes.

After a minute of this merry-go-round, he slapped my fore-head and knocked off my cap. I could do nothing but continue to back away from the dog. Then, he reached out and punched me in the arm, knocking the book out of my hand. I felt like the school-yard weakling about to get beat up by the bully!

In desperation, I looked out into the pathetic crowd and asked, "Are you guys going to stand there and watch this, or is somebody going to help me out with this dog here?" Nobody moved. I was astounded.

Minutes passed, and the young man's aggression kept increasing. He misinterpreted my constant running as a sign of my fear of him. It was as if his appetite to make good on his threats was increasing, and the growing crowd only added fuel to his fire. He was swelling with pride and power.

I, on the other hand, was embarrassed. I felt as though I was the featured fight at the school bus stop. The situation had become ridiculous, and I could do nothing about it. What the bully didn't know is that boys being boys, in years past, my friends and I loved to fight.

Without warning, he handed the dog to a friend in the crowd and charged toward me. I had no time to run, negotiate, or even move. I waited for his punch, and as it came at my face, I stepped to the side and landed a hard right just above his eye and followed up with a hard left into his other eye. His head flew back, and he stumbled into bystanders, who kept him from falling. Immediately a cheer rang out, and I looked in amazement at these spectators.

The loud-mouth held his hands over both eyes as he stumbled around. I backed away, wanting to have nothing to do with any of it. I reminded him, "Listen, I told you I didn't want to fight; I just defended myself!" He said nothing more. I picked up my hat and book and made my way through the crowd. Everyone gathered around, patting me on the back, telling me, "Great shot!" "Hey, you nailed that jerk!" and "I saw it all. That guy was attacking you!" I kept my head down and thought to myself, *Yeah, then why didn't you do anything about it?*

What is happening to our society? Why was this kid so irresponsible and violent? And why are so few willing to stand up for what's right?

I found it interesting that the owner of the Pit-bull became so angry and abusive when his dog attacked. After all, the animal was only doing what it had learned and what came naturally. Is there any question that the young man's violent behavior was also learned by example and grew because it was left unchecked?

I wonder if the parents of the children who witnessed our strange confrontation that day thought to take a minute or two to teach their kids something about what had happened. Were they just left to believe that such events were acceptable and normal for public gatherings?

Lately, society faces a terrible trend. Children are being taught lousy behavior through the words and actions of their guardians, and they are learning it from what surrounds them each day without parental intervention to illustrate what's best for them. Rarely does someone learn to have a positive outlook and a productive attitude without direct influence.

Consider the direction of many within my generation. One Generation X college student recently concluded a speech to hundreds of students with this statement, "...we now have nothing to look forward to!" He had just outlined the ills of society and explained how the previous generation's opportunities no longer exist. His words were received with applause.

Why did this audience of Generation Xers enthusiastically agree with such a dismal and limiting message? What does this say about the future of America?

Our Founding Fathers faced seemingly insurmountable odds at the inception of this great country. What would have happened if they had believed that it was too difficult to forge ahead and decided that there was nothing to look forward to in the face of opposition? Would we have ever known the freedoms that we enjoy and the opportunities that that freedom makes possible?

Many of my generation have accepted that they have, in effect, "...nothing to look forward to." The result? The slacker segment of Generation X. Misguided, disinterested, and hooked on MTV. Douglas Rushkoff, the author of *The Gen X Reader*, explained that Generation X (referred to as Busters) has been, *Born into a society where traditional templates have proven themselves quaint at best, and mass-murderous at worst. Busters feel liberated from the constraints of ethical systems, but also somewhat cast adrift. It must be nice to have something external to believe in. Having no such permanent icon (no God, no Country, no Superhero), we choose instead, by default, actually, to experience life as play and trust that the closer we become to our own true intentions, the closer we will come to our own best intentions. We see our increasing apathy as a strength and make a conscious effort to teach our compatriots how to remain liberated from the mind-numbing, hypnotic demagoguery perpetuated so successfully on everybody else. Whether you like it or not, we are the thing that will replace you.*

On the other hand, we find many Generation Xers who are seething with ambition and hope. One Generation X website, *JollyRoger*, reads, "We're proud to be the voice of the contemplating Generation Xers, inspired by truths higher than heroin, preferring thinking to drinking and mowing the grass to smoking it. We're cultural mutineers; guardians of common sense..."

In June 1997, *TIME* ran a lengthy article by Margot Hornblower on Generation X. Hornblower explains, "They (twenty-somethings) may be cynical about institutions, but they remain remarkably optimistic as individuals. At least half believe that they will be better off financially than their parents. And an astonishing 96% of Gen Xers say, 'I am very sure that one day I will get to where I want to be in life,' showing far more confidence than Boomers did a generation ago. For all their ironic detachment, today's young adults embrace an American dream, albeit one different from the vision their parents or grandparents had."

Without question, this is a fragmented group. Too young for any real accurate classification and too new to be understood entirely. But what Generation X certainly does share is this; we came up in a world of social decline and unstable foundations, which has heavily clouded the minds of many regarding an overall understanding of morality or the need for principle-centered living. Boomers raised most of us, and they didn't do much to improve our familial and social framework by their own admission. The same *TIME* article goes on to say, "...pollsters find that Boomers are markedly more pessimistic than Xers. Fully 71% of Boomers say, 'If I had the chance to start over in life, I would do things differently.'"

Mona Charen recently wrote, "We have engaged, since the great feminist revolution of the 1960s, in a wholesale retreat from child-rearing. The evidence is all around us that children are terribly damaged by the neglect they've suffered these past 30 years. Promiscuous divorce, illegitimacy, and, yes, overwork by parents have combined to *create a society in which children are left to raise themselves.*"

And so today, we are at a crossroads—a changing of the guard. The last of the Boomers are raising their children, and the Generation Xers are just starting their families. I wonder what my generation, a mixture of low ambition and bursting, unbridled enthusiasm, is planning to teach their children? Are they making any plans? And what are our present-day parents of teens teaching right now?

One thing I am sure of, though, is this: Most children eventually become as their parents are. Just as the Pit-bull took his violent lead from his master, children learn and carry on the "traditions of the fathers." And of late, many parents haven't been, well, going the extra mile!

The result today is that we are witnessing the perpetuation of the "If-it-feels-good, do-it!" attitude. It is all around us, and if this continues from generation to generation, we are headed for an excruciating and eventually irreversible social dilemma.

In his book *The Index of Leading Cultural Indicators*, William Bennett points out, "A disturbing and telling sign of the declining condition among the young is evident in an on-going survey. Over the years, teachers have been asked to identify the top problems in America's public schools. In 1940, teachers identified talking out of turn, chewing gum, making noise, running in the halls, cutting in line, dress code infractions, and littering. When asked the same question in 1990, teachers identified drug use, alcohol abuse, pregnancy, suicide, rape, robbery, and assault."

Societal decay is gaining momentum at a shocking rate. We see this downward spiral increase in pitch and velocity as if to foretell the probability of a complete flat spin soon. Our children face personal, familial, and educational problems far more complicated than we may have ever imagined. If this generational spiral is left uncorrected, the following generations will be left to stand alone, and lacking knowledge will undoubtedly perish.

Upsetting, yes. But we have not yet arrived at that point. Despite all that we see that is disappointing, our social problems are not irreversible. We are not in a flat spin, and I believe that the majority of the people in this world are trying to do what they believe is right. There is an abundance of happiness and opportunity to be found each day. Life in America remains full of many luxuries and possibilities, which cannot be found anywhere else in the world. As we experience this looming concern for the future of our society and the world, the need to begin making necessary and truly sufficient course corrections becomes urgent. It is now that we need to extend *Fair Warnings* to the next generation.

I'm a concerned parent and citizen. I have watched many peers stumble through life when perhaps some of their flailing's could have been avoided. As I have talked to many friends and acquaintances about the degree of guidance they received in their homes (and finding in some cases that leadership was virtually non-existent), I'm convinced that many specific familial changes are needed. There is an evident and urgent need for concerned and participating parents. Parents who are not only concerned with insisting their kids wear helmets when riding bikes, eat right, and avoid bad men in slow-moving vehicles but also insist their children are taught specific rules and truths about life. I'm talking about rules and principles such as honesty, hard work, positive attitude, and kindness. In short, we need great leaders.

Only after more leaders of families emerge and only after this change occurs will the Pit-bulls of American society, which threatens children's welfare, begin to lose their strength. Only then will we see more happiness in each home. Only then will more parents witness their children reach their full potential.

SECTION TWO:
The Role of Parents

CHAPTER 2:
The Most Powerful Position in America

The courageous man finds a way; the ordinary man finds an excuse.
—Anonymous

Recently on a talk show, a disgruntled mother complained about the recent release of new statistics indicating that drug use among teens is soaring again, reflecting nearly the high percentages of the '70s and early '80s.

"If this President hadn't been elected, this would have never happened!" she proclaimed.

"So, what you're saying," asked the host, "is that our President is solely to blame for our national drug problem?"

"Well, not solely," she answered. "But it's also the fault of the citizens who voted him in. I mean, after all, we do put him up there as our babies' example, don't we?"

Do we believe, whether we agree or disagree with a president, that he's responsible for Johnny's heroin problem?

Without question, the policies of an administration can significantly impact economic and national security issues. Social matters, however, are not so immediately influenced by an administration's policies. For example, while the ratification of the 13th Amendment in 1865 put an exclamation mark on the end of slavery, it did not change the hearts of oppressors. Racism remained a dominant mindset. Almost one-hundred years later, as black Americans yet suffered intense oppression, the Civil Rights Act of 1964 was signed, marking a positive move in the right direction. Yes, the laws are critical. But the pace of change and true racial equality can only happen as quickly as human-character improves. The roots of human-character, which grow into social outcomes, are planted within the walls of our homes.

Indeed, we should do our best to elect men and women who represent the good in America. We should attempt to elect those we honestly believe stand for correct principles. But do we put them on a pedestal as this good woman indicated "... as our babies' examples?"

Yes, political leaders have an opportunity to influence youth for good or ill. They have an impact on our social temperature depending upon the policies they accept or reject. However, there is no excuse for any parent in this country to blame politicians or school districts for their own children's problems, including teenage pregnancy or criminal activity. Political policies only add fertilizer to the roots of all individuals who are ultimately homegrown.

In the same vein, John Engler, Governor of Michigan, has stated, "The wisdom of the ages reveals that our moral compass cannot ultimately come from Lansing or from any other state capital, any more than it can come from the nation's capital, or Hollywood, or the United Nations. It comes from deep within us; it comes from our character, which is forged in our families and our faith and tempered in the arena of decision-making and action."

Every child is born pure. Although children do arrive with various genetic traits, none are born destined to succeed or fail. None are destined to a life of crime. None are destined to succeed. But all are guaranteed the opportunity for either. History is replete with stories of individuals born with all the worldly ease and comfort, who end up in prison or lead lives of self-inflicted scandal and controversy. Good looks, a proper education, and the financial independence to enjoy in a free country are not enough to breed a champion. Likewise, history is full of tremendous stories of individuals who began their lives in poverty and pain, yet rose to become great and contributing members of their society. They grew up on dirt floors. Some only attend school until the fourth grade because they had to work every day to assist their families. Their economic and social opportunities were severely limited. They were surrounded by hardship and crime. Yet, these people chose a course in life that was rich and fulfilling. They rose above their trying environment.

Why were these individuals able to succeed amid such opposition, while others met failure after growing up under ideal circumstances? I think of Howard Hughes, who was an American business magnate, investor, record-setting pilot, engineer, film director, and philanthropist. He experienced incredible financial success, public praise, and a glamorous lifestyle. Ironically, Mr. Hughes lived out his final days as a recluse. It is reported that he spent his days alone watching old films and passing the time in idle and destructive behavior. Hughes traded his handsome features for an unkempt beard and a frail, unfit body. He finally died quietly, alone, and admittedly miserable.

Why? Why was he not satisfied with all he had achieved? All the financial independence one could desire. Were his habits and depression too great to overcome? Why did he choose destructive behavior? Why did he fall to the depths of depression? Was it the President's fault? Did the schools fail to teach him about proper mental health and lifelong achievement? Did the public attention bring him down?

Ana Quirot was born in poverty in Cuba. Armed with a natural-born will to win, she became a national hero after winning the bronze medal in the 800-meter run during the 1992 Olympics. Becoming an Olympic medalist revealed her strength and depth of character. An unexpected accident later proved to magnify her deeper level of greatness.

While cooking in her kitchen in January of 1993, Ana was overtaken in a sudden grease fire, which quickly spread burning significant portions of her body. While in the hospital fighting for her life, she gave birth prematurely to a daughter who died after a week. This tragedy left her disabled, much of the tissue on her legs and arms severely burned. Her appearance was dramatically altered, and it was assumed that her career as a runner was finished. She may run again, some thought, but never at the world-class level. Ana thought otherwise.

Before this unforeseen event, Ana had set her sights on another Olympic competition. With this original goal, still in mind and relatively little time to prepare, she began a rigorous program to achieve complete rehabilitation. Seemingly unaffected by the odds stacked against her and willing to continue to feel beautiful despite her facial scars, Ana persisted confidently. She maintained the determination necessary to achieve her goal. To the astonishment of the world but probably not to those who knew her best, she did indeed achieve her goal. Ana began her comeback in November of 1993, running the 800 meters in 2:03.19 and placing second in the Central American Games. Again, she became the top in her country, winning the nationals in 1995. She represented Cuba in the 1996 Olympic Games and experienced the sweet satisfaction of realizing this magnificent and rare accomplishment.

How did she do it? And why? Who influenced her attitude toward life? Was it a communist government policy that taught her success? Did she receive a sizeable financial subsidy as her motivation? No.

Somewhere along the way, Ana and others who succeed learn a vital truth of life. This truth is that everyone is born with a gift to be used carefully throughout life. It is the gift of agency. It is the power to act for ourselves. We have the mental freedom to choose our way in life. Thoreau said, "I know of no more encouraging fact than the unquestionable ability of man to elevate his life by conscious endeavor."

Relatively few people have the physical ability and mental strength to become Olympic athletes. On the other hand, most people are blessed with the physical and mental capacity to create happiness and success.

We create joy or sadness based on our decisions and reactions to the circumstances in our lives. Except in the case of complete mental and physical incapacity, there is not a single situation in life in which we cannot decide what our reaction or response will be. These responses fashion our character or who we become. As we make productive choices day-to-day, our resolve is strengthened. Likewise, if we choose poorly, our ability to recognize and choose the good becomes limited.

Consider this insight from James Adams, "Let a man radically alter his thoughts, and he will be astonished at the rapid transformation it will affect in the material conditions in his life. Men imagine that thought can be kept in secret, but it cannot; it rapidly crystallizes into habit, and a habit solidifies into circumstance."

Whether our actions are good or bad, Ralph Waldo Emerson points out, "That which we persist in doing becomes easier. Not that the nature of the task has changed, but our ability to do has increased." Our habits, good or bad, become easier as we practice them.

If our parents or guardians don't understand this truth, how will it be learned? Are we going to wait and make vain attempts to teach these principles after our children are teens, and we see that we are losing them? Responding to a survey that I administered, a 20-year-old girl attending UC Davis indicated, "I feel that the best decisions I've made about my life have been the result of the values instilled in me by my parents."

Are we willing to risk the chances of our children learning the necessary principles in schools alone? Show me a school district that carefully and lovingly teaches these principles every day beginning in pre-school and extends the lessons through high school. They cannot. They're not intended for that purpose. I have heard of supposed unified school districts, none which provide the unity necessary to raise our children with consistent principled teaching. Sure, there are many fantastic instructors throughout the country. Loving, teachers, coaches, and religious leaders can have a lifelong impact on our children and even serve as a father or mother figure when the parents are not more available. Sometimes this happens, but in most cases, it's immature friends and others that become the over-riding influence in the absence of good parenting. We've all seen the results when children lead children or when adults without direction guide children down crooked paths.

Let's look at the principle of agency a little further to see how it creates a wealth of opportunity when correctly applied or weaves a web that binds when left unchecked and ignored. We're all aware of the difficulty of kicking a drug addiction. Nicotine ranks with heroin and cocaine when it comes to quitting. Each of us knows someone who abuses alcohol and hasn't found the strength to stop despite multiple attempts. Millions of smokers vow to kick their habit on New Year's Day. Most of those millions break their promise within two or three days.

Before getting caught in a hard-to-break habit, people choose to disregard an initial gut feeling. They ignore that whisper in their ear, which says, in effect, "You'd better not do this. This isn't the right thing to do!" We've all heard that little voice. Some call it a conscience. Others call it our Guardian Angel, The Holy Ghost, or The Spirit. While deciding to take that first puff, some may flatly ignore these promptings and later can't recall the initial, inner advice. Others may fight a little battle within their soul before choosing. They've been taught that they shouldn't experiment with cigarettes. They know it's terrible for them. Then, they make their choice. Our vices begin when we choose to ignore the initial warnings.

Over time, those who choose to continue smoking, for example, must force their way through the unpleasant coughing and gasping stage. Eventually, they're deaf to the whisperings, which initially warned them. Now their ability to step away and move in another direction is hindered. In time most clearly recognize the growing dangers of this habit. Some decide it's time to kick the habit. Much to their dismay, they find they're now facing not only a sizeable mental obstacle but also a physical one. Their bodies have become dependent upon the stimulating effects of their drug of choice. Their agency is weakened. The habit has been repeated so frequently that users feel like it's impossible to quit. Clinically, those habits are now addictions.

Addiction is usually linked to drug and alcohol abuse. I'd suggest that any destructive and compulsive behavior that we can no longer manage falls into this category.

Bad habits and addictions are always connected to temporary pleasure or gratification. "The high" is easy to obtain. With little effort, anyone can achieve the desired effect. Just inhale, swallow, or snort. It's simple. And so it goes with stealing, lying, gossiping, or violence. To steal, we pick up something we want and take it without paying for it. Lying is as simple as breathing itself. Violence happens with the mere swing of a fist. And feelings are torn with one sharp word. Alexander Pope penned it well when he wrote in his *An Essay on Man*:

> *Vice is a monster of so frightful mien,*
> *As to be hated needs but to be seen;*
> *But seen too oft, familiar with its face,*
> *We first endure, then pity, then embrace.*

As soon as we decide to involve ourselves in any form of negative behavior, we open the door to repetition. It becomes easier to repeat. The second drink is more comfortable than the first. The first theft is scarier than the next. The first time we angrily lash out at our parents, there's more adrenaline and fear than the second and third time. We set ourselves up for habitual behavior. We lose our sensitivity to our conscience and continue to weave a web of problems for ourselves.

Many wonder, while sitting in jail, a rehab center, unemployed, without friends, without family, without hope, "Why did this happen to me?" As more people ask that question amid self-inflicted dilemmas, this country's collective voice will soon whine in that same tone, "How could this have happened to us?"

Sir Winston Churchill once said, "A nation without a conscience is a nation without a soul. A nation without a soul is a nation that cannot live."

Many young people are left to realize the results of their behavior only after experiencing these hardships. They're enticed by the fun of drinking and drug use. They're drawn in by the thrill and ease of stealing. Teenage sexuality gives a false sense of maturity. It becomes second nature to show disrespect. And why not? Without anything else to look to, why wouldn't this be the natural course for many of them? It is all around them.

With the help of media and the mass of peer involvement, it all appears fun, especially for young people with little experience. And initially, it is fun. How does anyone possibly recognize the real danger and impact of their behavior without leadership from someone who knows?

Socrates wisely asked, "Whom, then, do I call educated? First, those who control circumstances instead of being mastered by them; those who meet all occasions manfully and act in accordance with intelligent thinking; those who are honorable in all dealings, who treat good-naturedly persons and things that are disagreeable; and furthermore, those who hold their pleasures under control and are not overcome by misfortune."

People who avoid addictive vices aren't left to complain, "Why did all this happen to me?" Happy, productive people made a conscious decision to move forward, not backward. They're educated about life. They have the presence of mind to follow their inner prompting to do what's right. They're willing to delay immediate gratification for long-term rewards. When they make mistakes, they're able to learn from them and begin to change. If bad habits are sown, they know there is no habit or weakness too great to overcome. They know that drug use can be curbed. Stealing, lying, and cheating are character flaws that can be overcome with determination. They understand that the difficulty of self-restraint and refusing temporary pleasure are necessary for growth, confidence, and happiness. They know they can choose to respond to any situation in a positive way. They control emotions and appetites at will. They are sure they can correct conditions when they have done wrong. They rise above their nightmares in life just as Ana Quirot could do. They were given *Fair Warning* early on and learned these valuable truths through the words and more significantly by the example of one or both parents.

The truth about the pathway to success or failure is depicted so well in the words of this anonymous quotation entitled *Habit*:

> *I am your constant companion. I am your greatest helper or heaviest burden. I will push you onward or drag you down to failure. I am completely at your command. Half the things you do you might just as well turn over to me and I will be able to do them quickly and correctly. I am easily managed—you must merely be firm with me. Show me exactly*
> *how you want something done, and after a few lessons I will do it automatically. I am the servant of all great men; and alas of all failures, as well. Those who are great, I have made great. Those who are failures, I have made failures. I am not a machine, though I work with all the precision of a machine plus the intelligence of a man. You may run me for profit or run me for ruin—it makes no difference to me.*
> *Take me, train me, be firm with me, and I will place the world at your feet.*
> *Be easy with me and I will destroy you. Who Am I? I am Habit!*

I was an unusually small kid. I looked like a large toddler up until the sixth grade. Nevertheless, I always sought out adventure. My older brothers, Greg and Chris, were always seeking ways to experiment and test their adventures on me. When I was about 11 years old, and Chris was 15, he and I came up with a neat idea.

In the garage, we found a cardboard produce box into which I could snugly fit. It seemed like we had found a perfect boxcar for me to ride in. We put the box on top of an old skateboard. Chris was going to give me a running push with a final heave-ho down our sloping cul-de-sac.

It was sure to be exhilarating. Exhilarating for me because of the speed and rushing wind and for Chris because of the element of danger with no physical risk for himself whatsoever. He didn't even need to coax me. I was eager for the thrill.

We put the skateboard in place at the top of the street. Alone with the road clear of moving vehicles, all systems were go. Chris held the box steady on top of the skateboard as I stepped in. My hips tightly slid in as I sat down. I settled in with my knees bent, pulled up close to my chest, arms wrapped around the front of my shins to squeeze nicely into the cardboard.... "cockpit." The top of the cockpit rose to my shoulders; only my little blonde head was visible. I was ready to ride!

I gave Chris the thumbs up, and he "started the engines." A slow jog at first to build momentum. His legs (my engines) ran faster as we hit a slight decline. I began to experience the thrill of our trial run. Soon, we were near full throttle. He gave that final burst of power, the old heave-ho. I would coast alone at top speed down the rest of the street, and hop out after our successful mission and sprint back to the top for another flight.

Before Chris' final heave-ho, unbeknownst to us, the cockpit had slowly rattled its way to the very front edge of the skateboard. With that last power burst, the cockpit took the plunge. Together, we lurched right off the front of the craft while traveling at top speed. Arms secured inside, I couldn't free them to use as a brace. Inertia entirely intact, our momentum met with a sudden thud. The weighed down cardboard meeting rough asphalt resulted in an even quicker halt. The texture of the cardboard eliminated any sliding possibility.

After the initial thud, as the street grabbed the cardboard upon impact, only one appendage was available as the final braking system to bring the disconnected bird to its final resting place. It was my skinny neck along with the sandy blonde head, which peered valiantly, wide-eyed, out of the cockpit. And the braking system I was. I ended the flight face-first into the pavement.

Luckily, I only suffered the loss of one or two layers of skin on my forehead, nose, and right cheek. To this day, I wonder how I didn't lose my nose altogether! Chris thought we should give it just one more try. I declined.

If we had been so fortunate as to have had an adult spying on us that day, I would have been spared some pain and suffering. I also would have had a more handsome school picture in my photo album from that year.

It's safe to assume that most responsible adults would have recognized the imminent dangers and done something to alert us. (Ironic, when we felt rather ingenious.) Just one quick comment from an adult might have caused us to step back and at least evaluate the project.

Still, I might have considered the frailties of our vehicle, but in the excitement of the moment, decided that "the show must go on." Then again, I might have considered these precautions and, out of concern for my well-being, made some modifications.

I could have somehow secured the box to the skateboard and tried a little test run down the driveway first. I could have freed my arms from being so tightly tucked around my legs, totally prohibiting any movement and greatly inhibiting balance. Whether I chose to heed the advice, my odds for success and added safety could have immediately increased 100-fold.

How many more dangerous, real-life situations will our children come up against? Whether they heed them or not, who is going to give the needed words of caution? Who really possesses the most powerful position in America? I say it's me. I have the most power in America. I'm just 26 years old, but I'm a father. Because of that responsibility, I wield the most significant influence in this country. If you are a father or mother or plan to be one, then you possess the same power. I accept the responsibility. I will not wait for others to do my job. I do not hold school districts or federal budgets responsible for the future of my children.

To an even higher degree, mothers, I believe, always carry more weight with their kids when they lead well because she carried them. She's simply mom. Together, parents make family decisions, which hold more weight than the numerous bills passed in majestic congressional halls. Over time, our correct decisions in family leadership will have more effect on our society's good than 100 social policies and dozens of State of the Union addresses.

Likewise, if I choose to abdicate my powerful position by neglecting to guide my children well, I'll play a significant role in the destruction of this country. I have the power to do that. I recognize that an overall societal and generational decline in character will destroy more than a nuclear holocaust or natural disaster.

As parents or future parents, together, we'll rejoice in our leadership results or weep with regret. We are the only ones who can teach a young child about the real dangers he/she inevitably will face. An occasional warning at school or church will not be enough to weather the constant, daily barrage of enticements our children confront. Good times and financial ease combined with casual instruction are not enough. Ten or fifteen-minutes of interaction with our children each day is not sufficient. No child care facility is qualified to bear your instructional responsibilities. Unexplained, unbending strictness does not breed obedience. Punishment without purpose does not produce trust. An abundant allowance of premature and unearned freedoms will create a loss of parental leverage. Acts of emotional, physical, and the most disgusting, sexual abuse turns a bright, gifted child to sadness and despair. These children find their ability to make correct decisions for a successful future hindered. The lives of their children are at risk even before birth.

Boyd K. Packer shares a story in a talk entitled, "Problems in Teaching the Moral Standard." "I recall on one occasion when I was returning to my home for lunch that as I drove in my wife met me in the driveway. I could tell from the expression on her face that something was wrong. 'Cliff has been killed,' she said. 'They want you to come over.' As I hastened around the corner where Cliff lived with his wife and four sons and his little daughter, I saw Cliff lying in the middle of the highway with a blanket over him. The ambulance was just pulling away with little Colleen. Cliff had been on his way out to the farm and had stopped to cross the street to take little Colleen to her mother who waited on the opposite curb. But the child, as children will, broke from her father's hand and slipped into the street. A large truck was coming. Cliff jumped from the curb and pushed his little daughter from the truck's path, but he wasn't soon enough.

"A few days later, I had the responsibility of talking at the funeral of Cliff and little Colleen. Someone said, 'What a terrible waste. Certainly, he ought to have stayed on the curb. He knew the child might have died. But he had four sons and a wife to provide for. What a pathetic waste!' And I estimated that that individual had never had the experience of loving someone more than he loved himself."

I believe most parents will sacrifice their lives to rescue or protect their children from physical danger or death in the heat of the moment. It's a natural reaction to jump into action when life-threatening events occur. Yet, many parents stand on the curb and watch as their children are mowed over before their very eyes. They're mowed over by the life-threatening obstacles and trials of life, which rush toward them each day. Because it's a more gradual tragedy, we procrastinate, rationalize, or altogether overlook the need to sacrifice ourselves on behalf of our young ones.

We may not be called upon literally to sacrifice our lives as Cliff was, but we must sacrifice much daily if we are to save the lives of America's youth. It is requisite that we live up to our position of power and stop wishing things to change. And stop worrying that other organizations do not provide adequate education and instruction. We must break the habit of looking to institutions to cure social problems and turn our attention to the real societal vaccine: familial self-reliance. We must be willing to sacrifice our bad habits and spend more of our time, talents, recreation, and excess leisure on behalf of our children. If we are to reverse our present course, we must learn to love our children more than we love ourselves.

As we do, our youth will consider the impact of their decisions with greater sensitivity and more often choose the good. Drug use will decline, racial equality will improve, violence will diminish, divorce will decrease, abuse will be curbed, economies will flourish, prison populations will fall, and welfare rolls will be rolled back.

May we wield our power wisely and take counsel from Henry David Thoreau, who said, "The fate of the country...does not depend on what kind of paper you drop into the ballot box once a year, but on what kind of man you drop from your chamber into the street every morning."

CHAPTER 3:
No Greater Joy, No Greater Achievement

When you want a thing bad enough to go out and fight for it, to work day and night for it, to give up your peace and your sleep and your time for it, if only the desire that makes your aim strong enough never to tire of it; If life seems all empty and useless without it, and all that you dream and you scheme is about it, if simply you'll go after the thing that you want with all your capacity, strength, and sagacity, faith, hope and confidence, stern pertinacity; if neither poverty, nor cold, nor famish and gaunt, nor sickness or pain of body and brain, can turn you away from the aim that you want, if dogged and grim you beseech and beset it, you'll get it!
—Berton Braley

A few weeks ago, a friend showed me an advertisement in a playbill for a popular play in the LA area. It was an ad for a well-known luxury car. Along with a beautiful picture of the car, the ad included a list of 20 of the most exciting life experiences. On the checklist is driving this vehicle. Other events on the list include 5. *Wear a suit made by a Seville tailor, 8. See the sunrise at Machu Picchu, Peru, 10. Fly on the Concord, 11. Stand on the Great Wall of China, 12. Make your own beer, 15. Take a balloon ride over the Serengeti, 17. Kiss passionately in public, and number 19. Ride the rapids of the Snake River in Idaho.*

All exciting and adventurous experiences. But are they really the most exciting in life? Why was there was no mention of the birth of a child, a baptism, or bar mitzvah? No reference to birthday parties, basketball games, and the ballet. What about the Tooth Fairy, Santa Clause, and Disneyland? No inclusion of prom night, graduations, college acceptances, engagements, and marriages. Nor any mention of anniversaries, family vacations, or reunions.

These are the experiences that should top any list. They're the significant milestones, the defining moments. Included in any family history, you'll find that these are the most important days, the fondest memories. In the great stories about these days, millions of families share stories about memorable individuals and situations, who add humor and uniqueness to events, making them spiritual and profound, but also fun, sometimes hilarious, and unforgettable. These experiences seem to perpetually overflow and lead to many long and oft-repeated reflections with friends and family, which begin with "*Remember when...?*"

Many of my own Generation X wanders through life without conviction or purpose, without direction, and being pessimistic about their future. It's due in part because of their parents' failure to demonstrate what brings lasting happiness. Parents failed to create a deep relationship with their children. What's more, they gave them premature freedoms.

For most of my Generation X friends, there's no shortage of fun and adventure in their lives. Many of them will soon face a great famine of substance when they must face life's real responsibilities. Left uncorrected, they'll remain adrift in this substantive famine for generations.

I once unwittingly experienced a similar famine first-hand. I am an above-average runner, a mediocre cyclist, and a sinking swimmer. So why not give a triathlon a try? That was my thinking three months before entering the Catalina Triathlon. I'm young and in shape. No problem. I subscribed to *Triathlete Magazine*. I logged many miles running. I cycled for hours. I swam lap after lap in the pool to achieve even the slightest semblance of buoyancy. The day arrived, and I took my bike, goggles, cap, and *Powerbar* to the island.

The entire scene was exciting. I registered, and they marked my number, 103, on my shoulders and thighs with that neat black ink. I felt official. Very athletic.

I was in the second wave of four to enter the water. We were to swim a little less than 1/2 a mile. A reasonably short distance compared to more rigorous events. My goal was to stay in the middle of the pack. The first wave jumped at the sound of the gun, and participants rushed down the beach and into the water. Splashing, kicking, just as it seemed when I watched the Ironman on ESPN. This was great!

Standing amid the group, cap secured, goggles in place, and Speedo snug gave me a feeling of accomplishment. Little did I realize that this was the highlight of the event for me. The gun sounded, I ran down to the water. I dove in and struggled to find a groove between the flailing arms of the competitors around me. Within the first 20–30 yards, I knew I was in trouble. In all my preparations, I had never really considered the vast difference between an 80-degree, 5-feet-deep pool, and the 63-degree, choppy, and bottomless ocean. I thought that all my years surfing for hours upon hours would have automatically qualified me for the elements. Was I ever wrong! I found that I could not keep my face buried in the water for any length of time as I swam because the cold temperature caused me to lose my breath. I had to look up and gasp for air continually. Defeated, I resorted to the breaststroke and backstroke, while attempting to relax and find a rhythm. My muscles began to cramp, and I soon found myself at the very tail end of my group. I was sure that I had seen 60-year-old men and women in my group. I tried to put that hard fact out of my mind!

By the end of the swim, I had been swiftly passed and brought up the rear, not of my group of swimmers, but of the third wave, who began their swim a full 10 minutes after us. I must have had some foresight as this was the first sporting event I decided to go alone, without family to cheer me on. Oh, what embarrassment I spared us all!

Legs like Jell-O, I walked up the beach to the changing area to prepare for the cycling. I honestly considered getting on my bike and slipping away into the hills of Catalina, find some cool shade and nap until my boat shoved off. But I knew I had to press on.

I was in the middle of the pack for the rest of the race. I suffered much of the same preparation famine as I had in the swim. Let's just say that my long flat rides at home did little to prepare me for the five grueling laps around the hilly island, which to me resembled the heights of Mt. Kilimanjaro. During the run, my proud 5 1/2 minute, single mile time turned to dragging 10–12 minute-miles. I ran mile after mile through a course of hills and valleys that felt like the Swiss Alps. Finally, I crossed the finish line feeling thoroughly exhausted, and so glad I had not brought a cheering section.

After what felt like 72 hours since arriving on that quaint little isle, I finally boarded the cruiser. As we headed back to Long Beach, I sat next to the window, stunned. I felt good that I didn't quit, but my athletic pride was squashed. I was nowhere near the athlete I thought I was. It took me about eight months before I could put my running shoes back on.

In hindsight, it's easy to see why this event was so difficult for me. Not only had I trained minimally, I had never attempted to combine all three events back-to-back in preparation. I only worked on each event separately. And so it is for the millions of people who grow up without needed instruction. They find themselves in a much more demanding world than they ever imagined. They come to realize that life is like a triathlon with many intertwined and connected events. To succeed, there must be a period of real training and conditioning. Not unlike triathlon training, "life-conditioning" in as many "events" as possible develops personal endurance so that individuals can weather the combination of circumstances in life.

Everyone is seeking happiness, yet many end up in despair. It is time we begin to teach the next generation where true happiness is found. Yes, it's a wonderful thing to seek success in education and career. It is noble to aspire to reach the top. It is good to be adventurous, travel the world, and experience the exciting moments in life. It is good to enjoy music, fashion, art, and entertainment. However, young people should understand that these alone will not bring complete satisfaction. They should learn that these life experiences are supplements to the more profound, lasting joy which comes from service to others, responsibility, time, and patience with family, kindness, and integrity.

Ask any of the great achievers in life what's important. Ask the movie star whose fame has dimmed, the athlete whose time has passed, the retired CEO, a past political giant, or a renowned professor. Most will agree that after the fanfare and the hoopla pass, the only happiness that genuinely endures comes from principles of service, integrity, and honor to faith and family.

Stuart E. Rosenberg expressed it well when he wrote, "Despite all new inventions and modern designs, fads, and fetishes; no one has yet invented, or will ever invent, a satisfying substitute for one's own family."

After the lights go down, most agree there is no greater joy and achievement than to attain love and happiness at home and to pass that formula to the children they love. With all his fame and recognition, our beloved President Abraham Lincoln had this to say concerning his success, "All that I am and all that I hope to be I owe to my angel mother. Blessings on her memory."

My generation and the next must come to know these truths. They will begin a course that they believe will lead them to happiness with or without us. And they can only learn from bitter experience or careful warning that many of the pathways that at first appear to lead to happiness only lead to destinations of disappointment. If they have no clear goals to look toward, they will go with whatever seems right, and will eventually get what they seek, good or bad.

I am convinced that consistent and straightforward teachings will provide valuable safety nets and lifelines for our youth. We can help many more of them attain success in life's milestone events. They will experience the joys of family and friendship, rather than repeating the struggles of the broken homes they may have come from. They will better cope with the trials and sorrows of life. They will learn to admit their errors and work to overcome them. They will know for themselves that the great achievements and joy in their lives have little to do with fortune or fame, but everything to do with faith, friendship, and family.

CHAPTER 4:
Fair Warning

If we work marble it will perish; if we work upon brass, time will efface it; if we rear temples, they will crumble into dust; but if we work upon immortal minds and instill into them just principles, we are then engraving upon tablets which no time will efface, but will brighten to all eternity.
—Daniel Webster

You have moved to the mountains and built your dream home on the bank of a beautiful, flowing river. One Saturday afternoon, you decide to head up that familiar trail to your favorite fishing hole. The oft traveled path bends through the canyon floor for about one mile before gradually ascending the canyon wall to the top of the dam. There, you find your small motorboat and shove off toward your secluded cove for an afternoon of fishing.

Unfortunately, today did not produce the desired catch. Two solid days of torrential rains and run-off created a lake of dark and unsettled murkiness. The lake is swollen to capacity, nearly 50 feet higher than any time during the last five years. The overflow of debris and sediment dashed all hopes of bringing dinner home.

Four hours later, it's evening, and you begin the descent into the valley walking adjacent to the dam itself. The water rushes from the opposite end of the dam and into the river. It fills your ears as its violent gushing echoes through the canyon. Louder and faster than ever before.

As you reach the base of the dam and begin to head down the river bed path through the trees toward home, a loud snapping, crackling sound from above startles you. Shielding your head, you crouch and quickly look up and behind you. It is dark, and you can scarcely make out the top of the dam. As you gaze up toward the structure's crest, you faintly hear what sounds like a rock bouncing off the dam's face and plunging into the water beside you.

Another cracking burst. More falling debris. Terror strikes your heart, and you feel your blood run cold as you realize what's happening. This dam is about to give way! You drop everything and begin to sprint through the woods toward your home. Your mind is racing. Ten minutes? One hour? How much time will we have to flee this canyon? Can I possibly make it in time?

Halfway to your home and family, you come to a grinding halt. The porch light of your only neighbor on the opposite bank beams into your wide eyes. They have no idea. Probably eating dinner and enjoying the evening together. Heart racing, you know you must sacrifice another five minutes to head deeper into the woods and backtrack a bit to the entrance of one of two bridges in the canyon. The river is now swelling, and you do what you know you must. You warn your neighbor. You save their lives.

Twenty minutes later, you and your family are safe and dry next to your neighbors, five miles downstream and on high ground. The valley is washed out, and both homes are gone. Yet, you've never felt more grateful.

I believe that such a hero lies within all of us. Most of us are willing to help in an emergency if we can do so. Most people will jump into action during a sudden life or death situation when no one else is there to help, even if it requires the sacrifice of their safety. Every day people across the country pull victims from burning homes, help at car wrecks, search for missing persons, and warn their friends and neighbors when disaster is coming.

We should be proud of our efforts and teamwork in these crises. Organizations jump into action to assist victims of natural disasters. Counselors swarm upon groups and individuals who have suffered at the hands of criminals. Drug rehab programs throughout the country help those who have ruined their lives with drug and alcohol abuse. Hotlines comfort the heavy hearts of those who are physically and sexually abused. I wonder how many of these crises might have been prevented. What if we were as effective at prevention as we are during an emergency?

Yes, many events cannot be easily foreseen. A car wreck. A natural disaster. A criminal act. And we do a pretty good job preparing for these unexpected, unforeseen events. We spend a few years pushing seat belt use. We have neighborhood crime watch programs. Smoke alarms and fire extinguishers are in every supply store. We put up security fences around the pool. We have taken preventative measures, but most of us still have that feeling that it won't happen to us and don't prepare as carefully as possible.

For instance, I purchased two 50-gallon drums a couple of years ago to store water in case of an earthquake or some other natural disaster. Very wise planning, don't you think? (Did you know about the mad dash for water during the 1995 Northridge, CA quake? Some store owners were convicted of price gouging.) Yet, the drums in my garage remain empty. In over two years, I have not taken 10 minutes out of my day to rinse them out, add some purifying solution, and run the hose into them. I park next to them every time I pull into the garage and think about filling them regularly and simply continue to put it off.

We must stop procrastinating. And while it's essential to prepare for life's environmental emergencies, it's even more critical to prepare for personal emergencies.

Let me explain. We spend some time preparing for the environmental emergencies that I've mentioned—things like natural disasters or accidents. But we also know that alcohol and drugs are as destructive as an environmental emergency, often even worse. They can lead to violence, theft, drunk driving, loss of employment, loss of family, etc. We all know that stealing and dishonesty can lead to years in jail, further crimes, and an overall loss of trust. We know that unbridled sexuality can ruin lives. We know that young kids are heavily influenced by what they see around them are very ignorant about potential consequences.

Yet, parents give their young children sips of beer at family picnics for a laugh. They encourage the excitement at turning 21 and being able to drink legally. Why such anticipation when the risks are so high? Is drinking alcohol so important that we should overlook the risks to satisfy the norm? Parents smoke in front of their children for many years. They go to the movies and buy tickets at the 12-year-old price for their 14-year-old kid. They call in sick to work when they are just sick of work. They yell at each other. They teach their kids to do as they do. They epitomize the oft-repeated phrase, *"Your actions speak so loudly, I can hardly hear what you're saying!"*

American evangelist Billy Graham observed, "We are preoccupied with material things. Our supreme god is technology; our goddess is sex. Most of us are more interested in getting to the moon than in getting to heaven, more concerned about conquering space than about conquering ourselves. We are more dedicated to material security than to inner purity. We give much more thought to what we wear, what we eat, what we drink, and what we can do to relax than we give to what we are."

Instead of setting the example, these parents think, hope, or assume that their kids will somehow still do better than they have done. Maybe they think their children will figure it out as they go along. It's as if the man in the canyon, while outrunning the oncoming disaster, decides to forego crossing the bridge to warn his neighbor. He figures they'll hear the water rushing through his yard, and that will be warning enough. Maybe he'll have enough time to escape.

Brett Easton Ellis wrote in an article featured in *George Magazine,* "It would be easy to be glib and condescending about the topic of kids in America, but things have changed drastically in the last 20 years, to the point where one can only really chuckle in grim disbelief. Cheating on exams? Smoking cigarettes? Shoplifting? You wish. Murder, rape, robbery, vandalism: the overwhelming majority of these crimes are committed by people under 25, and the rate is escalating rapidly."

He continues, "Given that the generation who raised this group of kids was so disconnected, so embroiled in its own narcissism, who can blame the kids themselves? We get the kids we deserve. And when your formative years are so sketchy, and you live in a world where drugs are as available as soda, and sex will kill you if it's not planned carefully; a world where divorce reigns; where your fear of violence is so paralyzing your classmates carry box cutters and guns to school; and then you pile on top of this world the usual set of adolescent anxieties, is it any wonder that kids either turn into computer geeks alienated from actual experience or retreat into the solidarity of urban gang life? What did we expect the outcome to be? Eddie Haskell?"

In the same article, Melissa Rossi quotes James Allen Fox, Dean of Criminal Justice at Boston's Northeastern University, who said, "We are facing a potential blood bath of teenage violence in years ahead that will be so bad, we'll look back at the 1990s and say those were the good old days." She also quotes Pulitzer Prize-winning author Edward Humes, whose book *No Matter How Loud I Shout* documents a year in the LA juvenile court. He says, "We have an army forming on the horizon. It's going to invade in the next 10–15 years, and we are not doing anything to defend ourselves."

Are we defending ourselves? I think Mr. Humes has a point. We must defend ourselves more effectively. Unless we're willing to tackle these problems head-on with real, sustained effort family-by-family across America, we'll find ourselves in a social free-fall. Not unlike the following story:

While en route, a small plane suddenly jolts and startles all aboard. Immediately the pilot tells the group that one engine has failed, but that everything is under control and will land safely within 30 minutes. Most ease back comfortably into their chairs. Again, the violent jarring is repeated. Quickly, the pilot affirms that another engine has been lost, but not to fear, the aircraft is still under control and will land shortly. Now, an overall tension permeates the entire plane. Another bout of sputtering and a third engine fails. Now most aboard begin to rustle, and some cry out in wonder and fear. At this point, both pilots emerge from the cockpit wearing parachute packs! The pilot raises his hand to get their attention. All are waiting for his instructions, and he says, 'Now don't any of you worry! We are going for help!' A hatch is quickly opened, and the two bailout together.

We just may find ourselves in such a position of powerlessness in the years to come. We must get ahead of it. When some of my friends developed an addiction to drugs or alcohol, I remember parents who didn't address them until they were out of control. These are the same parents who drove them to parties in the seventh grade, assuming they were playing pin the tail on the donkey and that other parents were running the night's activities. The parents weren't even home, and they had left plenty of liquor around the house while they had gone away for the weekend.

We are running a massive deficit in our effort to slow the growth of decadence. We hope to catch up with the problems now looming before us, but never give enough careful attention to the next generation. It's the next generation that can effectively and naturally slow the speed of social decay. This will only occur when far more Americans are willing to sacrifice the time and personal convenience necessary to raise a group of young adults who find better things to do than waste away in the now.

In the big picture, we only have a few years to be at home and learn from our parents or guardians. Most of my friends had one of two types of parents. The first and most ineffective type were the ones who let their kids experience practically anything. They had no objection to certain rowdy friends and gave virtually no direction or real care whatsoever. Most of the other kids saw these parents as "totally cool!" And then, there were the stricter parents who emphasized homework, sports, cheerleading, and other activities. These felt that if their child was active in sports and social events, received good grades and was accepted into a college, they had succeeded in raising a stellar child. Everything looks good on paper. These children were on their way to a successful future. Most likely, they would land a good job and end up making a stable income.

What about those raised by the second type of parents? Most would agree that they did succeed because their child pulled down good grades and went off to college. Furthermore, these offspring have an excellent chance of landing good jobs. But have those accomplishments alone really secured success for those kids? Everything looks good, but is it? What did they actually teach their kids? Did they cheat in school? Do they go to college and sleep around and cheat on boyfriends and girl-friends? Do they drink themselves into oblivion once they get there? Do they talk down to and about those with whom they associate? Do they think they are superior to another race? Is it possible that many of these kids are only postponing personal troubles? In their pursuit of knowledge, have they been ex-posed to or received any real wisdom from their parents?

Consider at the millions of individuals who have secured a solid education and gone on to be productive members of so-ciety but still suffer through the heart-wrenching consequenc-es of bad decisions. What of the hundreds of thousands in corporate America who sustain vicious addictions to alcohol, drugs, sex, and power. What of the hundreds of thousands involved in corporate crime, sexual harassment, affairs in the workplace, and racism? What of the hundreds of thousands who make solid, six-figure incomes because of their collegiate success, but have no relationship with their children and treat their spouses as secondary to money and prestige?

Don't our children deserve Fair Warning about these long-term obstacles? Don't they deserve parents who are willing to warn them and plead with them to avoid the mistakes they have made, and avoid the pitfalls only those experienced in life can reveal? Don't they deserve to have parents who are concerned with their children's ability to sustain the good life throughout their lives and not just until college graduation?

I consider myself one who certainly would have wandered down roads to terrible destinations if it hadn't been for the extra efforts made by my parents. I had every opportunity to do wrong, and I did my share of it. In fact, I was a rowdy kid. But during it all, I had clear-cut knowledge of right and wrong, which resulted in a healthy conscience. If I crossed certain barriers, I felt the sting of guilt. The more serious the compromise, the more acute the guilt became. I couldn't deny that I was veering off-course. Because of this knowledge of right and wrong, I had no excuses. My parents had already warned me. They didn't threaten me. They didn't shelter me. They weren't perfect and made plenty of mistakes, but they always explained the seriousness of right and wrong if something was a real threat to my future. They put up clear barriers for my safety.

Carefully read the words of the Englishman, Joseph Malins, who penned *A Fence or an Ambulance*, based on the adage, "An ounce of prevention is better than a pound of cure."

'Twas a dangerous cliff, as they freely confessed,
Though to walk near its crest was so pleasant;
But over its terrible edge there had slipped
A duke and full many a peasant.
So, the people said something would have to be done,
But their projects did not at all tally;

Some said, "Put a fence around the edge of the cliff,"
Some, "An ambulance down in the valley."
But the cry for the ambulance carried the day,
For it spread through the neighboring city;
A fence may be useful or not it is true,
But each heart became brimful of pity
For those who slipped over that dangerous cliff;
And the dwellers in highway and alley
Gave pounds or gave pence, not to put up a fence,
But an ambulance down in the valley.
"For the cliff is alright, if you're careful," they said,
"And, if folks even slip or are dropping,
It isn't the slipping that hurts them so much,
As the shock down below when they're stopping."
So, day after day, as these mishaps occurred,
Quick forth would these rescuers sally
To pick up the victims who fell off the cliff,
With the ambulance, down in the valley.
Then, an old sage remarked: "It's a marvel to me
That people give far more attention
To repairing results than to stopping the cause,
When they'd much better aim at prevention,
Let us stop at its source all this mischief," cried he,
"Come, neighbors and friends, let us rally;
If the cliff we will fence we might almost dispense
With the ambulance, down in the valley."
"Oh, he's a fanatic," the others rejoined,
"Dispense with the ambulance? Never!
He'd dispense with all charities, too, if he could;
No! No! We'll support them forever.
Aren't we picking up folks just as fast as they fall?
And shall this man dictate to us? Shall he?
Why should people of sense stop to put up a fence,
While the ambulance works down in the valley?"
But a sensible few, who are practical too,
Will not bear with such nonsense much longer;

They believe that prevention is better than cure,
And their party will soon be the stronger.
Encourage them then, with your purse, voice, and pen,
And while other philanthropists dally,
They will scorn all pretense and put up a stout fence
On a cliff that hangs over the valley.
Better guide well the young than reclaim them when old,
For the voice of true wisdom is calling,
"To rescue the fallen is good, but 'tis best
To prevent other people from falling."
Better close up the source of temptation and crime
Than deliver from dungeon and galley;
Better put a strong fence round the top of the cliff
Than an ambulance down in the valley.
(The Best Loved Poems of the American People [New York: Doubleday, 1936] pp.273–274.)

It's true that even as we build these fences for our families, some will climb over them. I know I sometimes did. Despite our best efforts, there will be children we work diligently to preserve who will go down dangerous roads. And each committed parent who has one of those determined to learn the hard way will at least be able to feel satisfied that they did all they could, thereby avoiding the deep regret that accompanies parental neglect. And for those few determined to choose dangerous paths, there will be thousands upon thousands more who easily could do likewise, but will be saved from a life of directionless agony because of the extra efforts and *Fair Warnings* they receive from their parents.

Individually, may we be mindful of the words of Marcus Aurelius, who writes, "A wrongdoer is often a man who has left something undone, not always that he has done something wrong." Collectively, may we be mindful of wisdom from Neal A. Maxwell, who warned, "A society that permits anything, will eventually lose everything."

In our struggle to help our youth acquire knowledge, we must remember not to neglect the more significant attainment of wisdom. Knowledge is fantastic and necessary. It's the critical learning about facts of history, science, technology, arts, religion, and politics. Wisdom is the more meaningful acquisition of the ability to reason, decipher, listen, and love. Wisdom also includes the ability to apply learning and experience in negotiating, maintaining self-control, extending compassion, and serving unselfishly. We cannot feel secure raising bright and knowledgeable youth without giving them the gift of wisdom.

Dwight D. Eisenhower said, "A man with knowledge and great moral principles is a great man; but a man with knowledge and no moral principles is only a clever devil."

This point is also put well by John Ruskin, who said, "Education does not mean teaching people to know what they do not know; it means teaching them to behave as they do not behave."

Henry Ford added his insight, saying, "An educated man is not one whose memory is trained to carry a few dates in history. He is one who can accomplish things. A man who cannot think is not an educated man; however, many college degrees he may have acquired. Thinking is the hardest work anyone can do, which is probably the reason why we have so few thinkers."

As we attempt to instill wisdom, this invaluable tool for life, we can raise a generation that will not leave the important things undone. We will have given them this Fair Warning and will have taught them much more than just how to get into a fine school, but how to become a fine person. They'll know how to think rationally and logically about the things that matter most. We will have crossed the bridge of personal sacrifice to warn them of the impending floods they will face in their lives.

In the first four chapters, I have attempted to establish a few critical points. First, we are in urgent need of healthy families led by great parents today. It's clear that if the quality and stability of family life doesn't improve within the coming years, we will witness the growth of insurmountable societal dilemmas.

Second, as parents, we possess more power and opportunity to change and save this country than any other individual or organization. Our children will eventually control the institutions which set agendas and create laws, just as the children of the Sixties, the Boomers, have a stronghold on these institutions today.

Third, we need to evaluate carefully and be willing to sacrifice the amount of time and effort we spend in pursuit of our social, occupational, and financial goals, which we expect will bring joy and fulfillment. We must realize that there is no greater fulfillment than that of a successful home and family.

Fourth, we know about life's dangers. We owe it to the children we have accepted stewardship over to extend the Fair Warnings, which will protect and benefit their futures.

In the following chapters, we'll look at some of the areas to which these Fair Warnings must be extended. I will share data, real-life personal experiences, and stories of others from my generation. The intention is to emphasize and shed new light on many things we are all aware of but may be leaving undone.

Some of what I have to say in the following chapters concerning the media, honesty, friendship, attitudes, alcohol, sex, and service may initially seem hard to digest. Some may feel that there is too much influence out there, and my suggestions are too strict or unrealistic. To those who think it can't be done, because kids will not choose to "say no" to certain things, I suggest that they underestimate the ability of youth to make good choices if they have the right amount of direction and loving encouragement.

I hope I can cut through much of the psycho-babble and get to the heart of things, which is this: We can and must lead our children to success by teaching, counseling, spending more time, showing more affection, building needed fences, and setting better examples. We decide that we will no longer stand aside and wait for an unlikely upswing in society; instead, we begin through a collective effort to positively force a change in our community. We can jump in with both feet knowing mistakes will be made and learning from them along the way.

Mark Twain once said, "The man walking down the street carrying a cat by the tail is gaining at least ten times as much experience as the man who is just standing there watching him."

We must do all in our power and make real sacrifices to avoid a tragic social fate. Laurence M. Gould explained it this way, "I do not believe that the greatest threat to our future is from bombs or guided missiles. I don't think our civilization will die that way. I think it will die when we no longer care. Arnold Toynbee has pointed out that, 'nineteen or twenty civilizations have died from within and not by conquest from without.' There were no bands playing and flags waving when these civilizations decayed. It happened slowly, in the quiet and the dark when no one was aware."

Tell me what you think so far!
Send me a direct message on Instagram:

@_fairwarning_
@jeffchavez_

SECTION THREE:
The Fair Warnings

CHAPTER 5:
Friends, Acquaintances, and Their Influence

*Every boy, in his heart, would rather steal second
base than an automobile.*
—*Midwest City Bulletin*

How many of your high school and college friends and acquaintances do you trust and depend on today? How many of them would you call on in a time of crisis? One? Three, or possibly five? The fact is, we lose touch with most of them, and those we do keep in touch with have little influence over us at this point. We grow apart as we make our way through life. We make new friends in our chosen professional fields and our new cities and towns.

Dig up an old yearbook. How many friends have you completely forgotten? Yet, these were the people with whom you spent most your time while growing up. You spent time with them in class, sports, cheerleading, recreation, parties, and practically every waking moment away from home. You spent hour upon hour with these people. These friends, whether many or only a select few, were unquestionably some of the most significant and powerful influences in your life. You heard the way they talked, and you talked like them. You saw the way they reacted and responded to countless situations, and you acted like them. You watched them make serious decisions about drinking, drugs, and sex, and you usually did what they did. You heard what they said about everyone else, and you said it too. Did they influence you for good or bad?

In most cases, upon honest reflection, your adolescent friends and acquaintances did little to help you become a better person. They usually wanted you to try all the fun stuff like smoking weed, ditching class, gossiping, and staying out all night. They wanted you to join them in every mischief. They contributed to the peer pressure of young life. I believe you will probably recall only a select few you say had an overall positive and constructive influence on you.

Consider some of the results of a survey, which I distributed to 200, 18–30-year-old college students:

Who or what was your most negative influence while growing up?

65% indicate that friends were their greatest negative influence.

20% indicate that parents or family members were their most negative influence.

15% indicate that TV and other miscellaneous sources were their most negative influence.

Who or what was your most positive influence while growing up?

58% state that their parents were their most positive influence.

22% state that their friends and siblings were their most positive influence.

20% state that religion and other miscellaneous sources were their most positive influence.

Has school or government ever influenced you to avoid early sex and drugs?

82% No
18% Yes

Were you ever taught how or why you should choose good, positive friends to hang out with?

62% No
38% Yes

It's interesting to note that 65% of those surveyed admit that their friends, the ones they loved to spend time with for all those years, were the most negative influence. Also, after all the rebellion and stress they gave their parents for enforcing all their do's and don'ts, the truth finally comes home to roost. Parents were, after all, the most positive influence on 58% of the participants.

The survey also suggests that schools and government have little effect on instilling moral behavior in young people, as 82% say they were not influenced by either school systems or the government to avoid detrimental conduct. In my opinion, the most significant statistic is that only 38% of these young adults remember any instruction or guidance from their parents concerning their selection of friends. Of note, schools do not significantly influence our kids morally; parents have the most significant positive influence, while friends have the least.

A good friend of mine might have avoided a terrible situation had he received a little parental counsel concerning his choice in friends.

We'll call him Alex Ruiz. He played Roadrunner football with me in the sixth grade. We were both tiny defensive backs who shared the same cornerback position. On occasion, his mom would drive us to the beach so we could surf all day together. She was a very cool mom. His uncle was a bass player for a world-renowned rock band and, Alex would often tell me about hanging out backstage whenever they played in the area.

When we entered junior high, we went our separate ways. We lived in different attendance areas. He went off to one school, and I headed to another. A few years later, I bumped into Alex again at a Friday night high school football game. We were both freshmen. Immediately, I noticed a dramatic change in my old friend. His head was shaved nearly bald, and he wore a plain white T-shirt and jeans with absurdly large military boots, which laced up just two inches below his kneecaps. It was apparent he was not as interested in seeing me again as I was seeing him. In our brief conversation, he mentioned he was moving to Colorado soon. Then, he quickly walked off with a similarly dressed friend. I thought very little about the meeting.

As I opened my locker between classes during the first semester of my sophomore year, a friend walked up and handed me the latest edition of *Time Magazine*. The cover featured mug shots of four teenagers under a bold headline, *AMERICA'S MOST WANTED TEENS*. In the bottom, right corner was a picture of my old friend, Alex Ruiz, head shaven, stony-faced with blemishes. I turned to the article in stunned amazement and read how Alex was wanted for murder in Denver, Colorado. Now a member of a racist skinhead group, he and two others had lain in wait for a gay hairdresser. When he left the salon, he was brutally beaten by the three young men, set aflame, and then dumped into a nearby creek.

I can't help wondering what his fate might have been if we had gone to the same schools. I wonder what concern, if any, was shown by his mother when she noticed the visible signs of change: the clothing, his new look, and the less than social friends. How late was he out each night and with whom? Were there any rules? Had she been enforcing guidelines over the years?

There's a story about an independent, little, nine-year-old boy who announced to his mother and father one night at the dinner table, *I am running away from home tomorrow. Who's going to drive me?* Children are innocent and powerless to undertake even the smallest of tasks without help. For many years, they are forced by their limitations to learn from their parents. Due to this awesome responsibility, it's incumbent upon us, as parents, to keep our children involved in wholesome and productive activities and know where they go and with whom.

We're not talking about paranoid shelter here. We're talking about reasonable, loving guidance. Everyone on this earth will have associations with so-called bad influences. I suggest that most parents would be shocked to see all the compromising individuals and situations their children are regularly subjected to, starting at a very young age and in the most unexpected places. As little children, they all meet the friend who teaches them their first swear words, shows them their first dirty picture, teaches them how to hold a cigarette, persuades them to steal a pack of gum, encourages them to pick a fight, and so on. It occurs on the playground, in friends' homes, in the classroom, at Little League games, and in the neighborhood park.

We recognize that our kids inevitably will be exposed to these people, and these situations probably sooner rather than later. It's a necessary part of life to meet these individuals and circumstances head-on. We all must learn to deal with the different types of people and situations that we face in life. It would do us no good to try and shelter our children from the world. This process of exposure builds character and social maturity if handled correctly. Parents must see that their children are not unnecessarily over-exposed. Children cannot be allowed to spend countless hours of unsupervised, idle time with unfamiliar or shady kids. They must be supervised so they can find the balance between minimal exposure and detrimental over-exposure. It would be impossible, unhealthy, and unwise to shield our children from everyone who might persuade them to do wrong. They need the opportunity to exercise their freedom of choice and fall occasionally, then with your help, pick themselves up and try again.

Case in point: During my fourteenth year, I finally received the package I had been waiting eight weeks to arrive. My eyes fixed on the only word which mattered in the entire letter, "Congratulations!" I was going to Mexico, and I was elated!

I was one of 15 teenagers representing the United States in a foreign exchange, Freestyle, and Greco–Roman wrestling tournament in Mexico City. I qualified after competing in a series of tournaments during the 1986 spring wrestling season in Southern California. I would represent my country in the intimidating 88-pound weight class.

All the necessary legal and organizational arrangements were made, and the time had finally come. We spent six days in

Mexico City until the end of the tournament. We then flew to Cancun for an additional five days of sight-seeing and relaxing in the sun. All appeared well and good, and I am sure my parents were just as excited to send me as I was to go.

When we arrived at the hotel, we were given maps of the area by our three coaches. This was virtually the last time I saw those men. We were given the schedule, and then we were left on our own from that point forward. We saw our vacationing coaches only at the tournament sight, on one or two planned tours and at the airport. Surely, this amount of free reign had not been explained in the original itinerary. The next 11 days proved to be the most eye-opening, innocence-shattering experience of my life.

Pete, 17-year-old, born and raised in Los Angeles, was the only one who spoke Spanish. He became the team's nightlife leader. "Taxi!" he yelled out. It was about 8:00 pm, and all 15 of us piled into two taxi cabs. I squeezed into the front seat next to Pete. "Donde?" asked the old man. "Red light district," came the excited reply. *Red light district...* I thought about those words. I had heard that phrase somewhere before. I couldn't recall what it meant exactly, though. An arcade? Maybe a laser show? I wasn't sure. Everyone seemed excited. I was having a lot of fun.

We pulled off the main street and headed down a dark alley. We parked next to a trash bin, and the taxi cab driver gave what I sensed was some sort of specific instructions. Everyone was quiet, and Pete leaned back and said, "Now, all of you just shut up and follow me. Don't make any noise." Then, he looked over at me and said, "Chavez, you stay here with Ramsey; we'll be back in about an hour." They all left, including the taxi drivers.

There we were—Ramsey (our destructive 105-pounder) and me, (88 pounds of prowess) in a dark alley somewhere in the middle of Mexico City. We still weren't sure what kind of red light game they were playing up there; we only knew that we were scared out of our wits as we sat there, alone, slumped down in the back seat of the cab.

After watching two or three men stumble down the alley past us, we decided it was time to get out of there. When the coast was clear, we scrambled down the littered alley, around a large building, and up five flights of steel stairs with no railing and were lit with a red bulb at each landing. The stairway ended, and we were looking down a dark hallway that led to a large, red, smoke-filled room. We found our teammates sitting at a table in the corner, laughing and drinking. The room was filled with the most under-dressed women I had ever seen. These ladies were strutting around the room and hanging on the shoulders of some of the men. All at once, I knew exactly what the red light district was, and I could hardly believe I was there.

After about an hour of watching my team drink each other under the table, Pete, our brave leader, suddenly appeared sauntering toward us from a dark corridor. He acted as if he had accomplished something worthwhile with a trashy lady on his arm and a sneaky smirk on his face. None of the other guys had the money required for a "purchase," so we all got up to leave. At that point, the brothel's proprietor pulled out a large pistol, bellowed a loud, rolling Spanish curse, and stood in front of the only exit. Ramsey and I began to cry like babies.

The crook wanted payment for the two bottles of tequila he had initially offered as a gift. He was demanding the special "Americano" price of just $50 per bottle. We had only $30 among us. I thought I would be killed right there, just 14 years old, in the middle of a whorehouse over an unpaid liquor bill.

Our taxi cab driver acted as our mediator and continued to point toward Ramsey and me as we wept for our lives in an attempt to solicit sympathy from this corrupt man. After over 30 minutes of negotiations, he finally relented taking all our money and giving a quick wave of his gun as the signal for us to get out. We were out the door, down the stairs, and dove headfirst into the two cabs.

We made it back to the hotel that night and every night after that by what seemed like the skin of our teeth. Lacking the courage to just stay home by myself each evening, I was dragged about the streets and through the bars of Cancun during the remaining nights. I heard some of the guys' brag about the results of their sex contest: who could have the most sex before going home. I witnessed the fights, the drunken vomiting, and the overall mayhem that went on every night of the trip. Finally, I arrived home with a tanned body, two shiny tournament medals, and a whole new perspective.

It would be many years before I told my mom and dad about the details of that trip. They had no idea we had been left to ourselves the way that we were. Since there were no red flags to indicate the total lack of supervision that would justify keeping me home, I had been allowed to go and reap the rewards of my efforts and be trusted.

I share this experience to point out that there will be scores of compromising events and people who will enter the lives of your kids while they are away from your immediate influence. These events will arise even after you've done all in your power to ensure they are out of harm's way, as my parents did before this trip. Once on their own, all they will have to direct them is their conscience and what they learned about right and wrong at home. Why then, would you not monitor and influence the time and whereabouts spent with certain friends? Why not make an extra effort to get to know your children's friends? Find out for yourself if they are a good or bad influence on your child. Why not teach your children to choose positive friends and limit the number of compromising situations they will have to face?

Pete had not received a whole lot of guidance in his life. He was like loose cannon when allowed to choose for himself. Pete fits the classic profile of the group leader who always has that bright idea, which was nothing but trouble. It was as if he had waited his whole life to be out on his own and experience the world's darkest corners.

In retrospect, I recognize that most of the other guys were experiencing many of these temptations for the first time themselves. Ramsey avoided involvement only because he latched on to me. Then, he could avoid the pressures of experiencing things he was so obviously afraid of at 14 years. I wonder if he had another friend to help him in a year or so when the next opportunity presented itself.

Over the years, I have watched a few of these guys, including Pete, remain close friends, wrestle on the same college team and room together. I wonder if they ever did clean up their acts. Keeping each other as constant company, their odds of mellowing were probably very low, their chances of continuing their dangerous mischief indeed remained high.

Ex-con Harold Morris has spent nearly 20 years warning young people to avoid the snares that nearly destroyed his life. In his well-circulated video presentation, Twice Pardoned, Harold talks about the perilous effects of peer pressure and how little mistakes can have significant consequences.

As a young man, Harold was an All-American athlete with many scholarships available to him. He relates his experience of choosing to run with the wrong crowd and how that choice altered his life forever. After making new friends at a night club, Harold found himself behind the wheel of the getaway car after his two new associates robbed a store and fatally shot the attendant. He had no prior knowledge of their plans to commit these crimes. Within one year, Harold was arrested and given two life sentences for armed robbery and murder. His conviction hung on the sworn testimony against him from the two friends who had committed the crimes themselves.

He spent over ten years behind bars, which ended when he received a miraculous pardon. Over the years since his release, Harold has talked to thousands of young people about his experience. When referring to his false imprisonment, he tells them, "Now don't you feel sorry for me! I consorted with the scum of the earth, and I became as they were. I tell you today that who you associate with in life will determine the outcome of your life, good or bad. Please know that! You must be selective about who you choose to associate with. You choose a group that's going somewhere."

Similar situations and others far more sinister happen every weekend in every city in America. Young boys and girls are coerced and even pushed into unwanted sexuality. Elementary and junior high kids are continually offered alcohol and the most sophisticated, addicting forms of other drugs. Fighting, stealing, racism, and cheating run rampant. Simple logic tells us that the fewer times a person is in the presence of such activities, the less his/her chances are of becoming involved. We need to remember that if our social development, particularly in the early and teenage years, is mismanaged, the negative repercussions may last a lifetime. We do become that which we associate with most.

A youth leader once told me, "A friend isn't a friend who will ask you to do something wrong. They are just acquaintances." I didn't get that phrase for many years. I had plenty of friends who tried to get me to do sketchy things. They were a lot of fun to hang around, and they were part of a popular crowd. Ten years later, I don't know where most of them are, and they've never made any attempt to keep in touch with me, their old friend. It's only now that I realize how many hundreds of acquaintances I had compared to the handful of friends who remain.

It's sad to see the great lengths kids will go to please the acquaintances they innocently mistake for friends. It's heartbreaking to see the great lengths young boys and girls will go to satisfy the boyfriend or girlfriend whom they mistakenly view as the "only love" of their lives.

Recently, there was a report of a teenage couple who were allowed to spend nearly every waking moment together. When the parents realized that their excessive amount of time together hindered education and social activities, they put a stop to it. Unwilling to be apart, these two kids tragically and dramatically took their lives by jumping into a waterway in a vain attempt to be together forever.

Initially, kids don't have the experience required to differentiate between friends and acquaintances or true love and infatuation. Learning to understand the differences between each and learning how to identify and appropriately deal with each is a Fair Warning all youth deserve to receive. Having this Fair Warning could have helped many of my friends reach their potential rather than spend years stumbling around. Nearly all my friends who faced serious personal trouble were those who had been allowed to run with whomever they wanted, whenever they wanted, wherever they wanted.

Kids thrive when there's a productive schedule at home. They excel with involvement in sports, music, church programs, part-time jobs, and other worthwhile extracurricular activities. Within these activities, kids meet others who, with their parents' support, are choosing to succeed. They, too, will become achievement-oriented. Further, they'll take these experiences into adulthood and have developed the wisdom to choose good friends and associates in their professional, financial, political, and business pursuits.

Believe it or not, one day, your little ones will reflect in gratitude for parents who enforced curfews, kept tabs on their whereabouts, and knew their friends and acquaintances from their earliest social development.

I knew my old friend, Alex Ruiz, well. He was not born a murderer. He became one. He could have become an architect, a school teacher, or a policeman. He might have become a wonderful father. He had great potential. I can't help but wonder what price he would pay today to relive his youth and pick a new group of friends. How many people throughout the country would give up everything they now possess to start again and live life knowing how to choose peers and partners?

CHAPTER 6:
Attitudes

*Nothing on earth can stop a man with the right attitude from reaching
his goals. And nothing on earth can help the man
with the wrong attitude.*
—*Thomas Jefferson*

"The little country schoolhouse was heated by an old-fashioned,
pot-bellied coal stove. A little boy had the job of coming to school
early each day to start the fire and warm the room before his teacher, and his classmates arrived.

One morning they arrived to find the schoolhouse engulfed in
flames. They dragged the unconscious little boy out of the flaming
building, more dead than alive. He had major burns over the lower
half of his body and was taken to the nearby county hospital.

From his bed, the dreadfully burned, semi-conscious little boy
faintly heard the doctor talking to his mother. The doctor told his
mother that her son would surely die, which was for the best, really,
for the terrible fire had devastated the lower half of his body.

But the brave boy did not want to die. He made up his mind
that he would survive. Somehow, to the amazement of the physi-
cian, he did survive. When the mortal danger was past, he again
heard the doctor and his mother speaking quietly. The mother was
told that since the fire had destroyed so much flesh in the lower
part of his body, it would be almost better if he had died since he
was doomed to be a lifetime cripple with no use at all of his lower
limbs.

Once more, the brave little boy made up his mind. He would not be a cripple. He would walk. But unfortunately, from his waist down, he had no motor ability. His thin legs just dangled there, all but lifeless.

Ultimately, he was released from the hospital. Every day, his mother would massage his little legs, but there was no feeling, no control, nothing. Yet, his determination that he would walk was as strong as ever.

When he wasn't in bed, he was confined to a wheelchair. One sunny day, his mother wheeled him out into the yard to get some fresh air. This day, instead of sitting there, he threw himself from his chair. He pulled himself across the grass, dragging his legs behind him.

He worked his way to the white picket fence bordering their lot. With great effort, he raised himself upon the fence. Then, stake by stake, he began dragging himself along the fence, resolved that he would walk. He started to do this every day until he wore a smooth path all around the yard beside the fence. There was nothing he wanted more than to develop life in those legs.

Ultimately, through his daily massages, iron persistence, and resolute determination, he did develop the ability to stand up, then to walk haltingly, then to walk by himself—and then—to run.

He began to walk to school, then run to school, to run for the sheer joy of running. Later in college, he made the track team.

Still later in Madison Square Garden, this young man who was not expected to survive, who would surely never walk, who could never hope to run, this determined young man, Dr. Glenn Cunningham, ran the world's fastest mile!"

(Chicken Soup for the Soul, *as told by Burt Dubin* [1993], pp. 259)

If such incredible obstacles can be overcome, just think of the many common imperfections of humanity that can be overcome with the right attitude. We all know someone who, if only they exhibited a more positive attitude, might do and be much more. These types of individuals would then be living their dreams. They would have more friends and a more meaningful life. M. Russell Ballard said, "Remember, a good attitude produces good results, a fair attitude fair results, a poor attitude poor results. We each shape our own life, and the shape of it is largely determined by our attitude."

How we view certain obstacles or day-to-day tasks greatly determines our moods, effectiveness, stress levels, successes, and relationships. Consider how, after being cut-off on the freeway, many people arrive at work in a terrible mood. The tone of their entire day has been set and eventually experienced by everyone around them. When asked how things are going, they respond, "Horrible!" or "Oh, it's been one of those days!" Many others refuse to be affected by things like this and don't dwell on circumstances beyond their control. These individuals arrive at work with a pleasant attitude and continue to enjoy the day and remain effective as they handle their responsibilities.

Each year, millions rapidly change their lives from mediocre at best to highly successful and deeply meaningful. They do this with a mere change of attitude. They come to the sweeping realization that events and circumstances do not control us, but our emotional responses to daily situations determine our successes and happiness.

I was blessed to learn these truths at a very young age. It didn't immediately sink in, but I eventually learned what my parents were trying to teach me. Dad would come home, look at the scowl on my face, and ask, "Why are you in such a nasty mood?" I would reply in a huff, "Because Chris and Greg are making me mad!"

"What do you mean, 'making you mad?'"

I would then complain, "Chris keeps pinching me, and Greg took the remote control away."

Before saying a word to the accused, my dad would say to me, "Then, why don't you get away from them and go do something else? Don't just sit there and let yourself be mad."

Planned or not, Dad taught us very early on that we can change our circumstances and moods, which affect our overall attitude, by merely realizing our situation and doing something about it. In this case, I could get up and leave.

This teaching opportunity did not provide me with the solution I was seeking, but rather, the answer I needed because life's best solutions do not always come the way we want them to. After all, I was the one being pinched and intruded upon. Why should I have to get up and leave? Because I could change my circumstances. Learning to adjust when in uncomfortable situations is much more valuable than trying in vain to make each condition comfortable.

I was beginning to learn that many unpleasant circumstances in life are completely out of our control. We must face these challenges head-on; we need to deal with them. This requires a higher level of self-control. It requires the ability to choose to be resilient and productive despite difficult circumstances.

In one of his talks, Vaughn J. Featherstone related this critical lesson, "Years ago, Russell LeBaron Briggs, while Dean of Harvard Law School, gave a speech. He told of a student who came in one day, and the Dean asked him why he had not been there the day before to take a test. The student said, 'I wasn't feeling very well, sir.' Dean Briggs said, 'I think you will find, my young friend, that in life most of the work in the world is done by people who are not feeling very well.'" It's this ability to control our attitude even when we aren't feeling like it, which separates the truly great ones from the masses.

What will you do when life's difficulties have been heaped upon you, and you feel hard-pressed even to muster a smile? Will you allow that feeling to take control and lead you into a state of depression? No. You can make a choice.

Psychologist and philosopher William James put it this way, "Action seems to follow feeling, but really action and feeling go together; and by regulating the action, which is under the more direct control of the will, we can indirectly regulate the feeling. Thus, the sovereign voluntary path to cheerfulness, if our cheerfulness be lost, is to sit up cheerfully and to act and speak as if cheerfulness were already there."

It's interesting to note that two people may be in the same place, doing the same job for the same company, earning the same income, and living in the same neighborhood in the same city, yet one is miserable and the other happy. Why? Because of their different mental attitudes. We can find just as many smiling faces doing back-breaking work in rice fields as we can in the high-income, air-conditioned offices of Los Angeles and New York.

"There is nothing good or bad," said Shakespeare, "but thinking makes it so."

Abe Lincoln once proclaimed, "Most folks are about as happy as they make up their minds to be."

In the classic book, How to Win Friends and Influence People, Dale Carnegie shares this story, "I saw a vivid illustration as I walked up the stairs of the Long Island Railroad station in New York. Directly in front of me, thirty or forty disabled boys on canes and crutches were struggling up the stairs. One boy had to be carried up. I was astonished at their laughter and gaiety. I spoke about it to one of the men in charge of the boys. 'Oh yes,' he said, 'when a boy realizes that he is going to be a cripple for life, he is shocked at first; but after he gets over the shock, he usually resigns himself to his fate and then becomes as happy as a normal boy.'"

A wonderful father, successful businessman, and president of a stake or area in the Church of Jesus Christ of Latter-Day Saints, Jack Rushton has been loved and admired by thousands over the years, known not only for his leadership skills and devotion to his beliefs but also for his great sense of humor and personality.

Thousands now know Jack for his stellar example of how to
move on and achieve greatness through service and inspiration
despite life-altering injuries.

One day while enjoying an afternoon with his family in
Laguna Beach, California, Jack body-surfed a small, seemingly
harmless wave toward the shore. Unexpectedly, the swell picked
him up and drove him into the sand headfirst. Since that day,
he has been completely paralyzed from the neck down.

After lying unconscious for several weeks in the hospital,
Jack finally came to and peacefully gazed up at family and
friends. At this point, all were anxiously waiting for any sort
of communication. Everyone quietly gathered around his bed
to hear what his response to this terrible life sentence might
be. With great effort and without expression, Jack mustered, in
strained tones, the following:

"My-- name--is---Jack. I---broke--my--back!" A beautiful
grin stretched across his face. Family and friends laughed and
cried with great relief. Jack was back!

From that day to this, Jack Rushton has indeed been back.
He is even more influential and inspirational than before. His
cheerful attitude amidst such a trial has helped others reach
beyond themselves and become great as well.

A group of church members and neighbors pitched in time,
talent, and resources night and day to build a beautiful addition
to Jack's home to meet his unique needs. Many others sent
letters and expressions of love and encouragement. The good
friend who served at his side during his ministry as a stake
president continues to visit him every Thursday as he has for
the last six years. And there is the massage therapist who vol-
unteered to massage Jack's feet regularly, to whom Jack once
joked, "It is so nice of you to do that for me. It sure looks like
it would feel really nice too!"

And then there is his wife, who, without complaint, serves
him day and night—washing, dressing, feeding him, and attending to all his strenuous and highly specialized needs.

Jack Rushton's resilient attitude, combined with service, has proven to edify everyone around him. He inspires others to readjust their attitude about their present situation, whatever it might be.

To illustrate just how a change of attitude in day-to-day responsibilities can change a life forever, I share the story of Jean Thompson as re-told by Vaughn J. Featherstone:

On the first day of school, Jean Thompson told her students, 'Boys and girls, I love you all the same.' Teachers lie. Little Teddy Stollard was a boy Jean Thompson did not like. He slouched in his chair, didn't pay attention, his mouth hung open in a stupor, his eyes were always unfocused, his clothes were messed, his hair unkempt, and he smelled. He was an unattractive boy, and Jean Thompson didn't like him.

Teachers have records. And Jean Thompson had Teddy's. First grade: 'Teddy's a good boy. He shows promise in his work and attitude. But he has a poor home situation.' Second grade: 'Teddy is a good boy. He does what he is told. But he is too serious. His mother is terminally ill.' Third grade: 'Teddy is falling behind in his work; he needs help. His mother died this year. His father shows no interest.' Fourth grade: 'Teddy is in deep waters; he is in need of psychiatric help. He is totally withdrawn.'

Christmas came, and the boys and girls brought their presents and piled them on her desk. They were all in brightly colored paper except for Teddy's. His was wrapped in brown paper and held together with scotch tape. And on it, scribbled in crayon, were the words, 'For Miss Thompson from Teddy.' She tore open the brown paper and out fell a rhinestone bracelet with most of the stones missing and a bottle of cheap perfume that was almost empty. When the other boys and girls began to giggle, she had enough sense to put some of the perfume on her wrist, put on the bracelet, hold her wrist up to the children and say, 'Doesn't it smell lovely? Isn't the bracelet pretty?' And taking their cue from the teacher, they all agreed.

When all of the children had left, Teddy lingered and came over to the desk and said, 'Miss Thompson, all day long you smelled just like my mother. And her bracelet, that's her bracelet, it looks real nice on you too. I'm really glad you liked my presents.' And when he left, she got down on her knees and buried her head in her hands and she begged God to forgive her.

The next day when the children came, she was a different teacher. She was a teacher with a heart. And she cared for all the children, but especially those who needed help. Especially Teddy. She tutored him and put herself out for him.

By the end of the year, Teddy had caught up with a lot of the children and was even ahead of some. Several years later, Jean Thompson got this note:

> *Dear Miss Thompson:*
> *I'm graduating, and I'm second in my high school class. I wanted you to be the first to know. Love, Teddy*

Four years later, she got another note:

> *Dear Miss Thompson:*
> *I wanted you to be the first to know. The university has not been easy, but I like it. Love, Teddy Stollard*

Four years later, there was another note:

> *Dear Miss Thompson:*
> *As of today, I am Theodore J. Stollard, MD. How about that? I wanted you to be the first to know. I'm going to be married in July. I want you to come and sit where my mother would have sat because you're the only family I have. Dad died last year. Love, Theodore.*

And she went, and she sat where his mother would have sat because she deserved to be there.

This good teacher's willingness to gather her thoughts, reassess her perspective, and make a conscious decision to change her attitude changed a life forever. Sadly, many people do not realize the potentially life-altering effects of the most basic attitude adjustments. Many people equate a positive attitude only with dramatic recoveries, financial success, or publicized accomplishments.

Attitude is more than that. Attitude is the key to success or failure in all that we do, good or bad, including how we face the most common social dilemmas of the day. It affects the quality of our day-to-day lives. It determines how we live and how we behave. Our attitude shapes our goals and our dreams. It affects all of our relationships, including whether we choose to treat people kindly or not. Attitude can unleash our highest potential or hide it, as it were, ...*under a bushel.* Our attitude toward everything we do in life determines our overall happiness.

Consider a broader look at the effects of a good or bad attitude. Children who are not explicitly taught to cultivate a positive and resilient attitude will make many unnecessary blunders as they experience life. These blunders have the potential to become serious.

As an example, attitude is at the root of hiring and firing within most companies. The first one hired, and the first one fired, has almost everything to do with attitude, reflected in demeanor and self-confidence.

Attitude lies at the root of violence as well. Children and adults who engage in any form of violent behavior do so because of an extremely negative attitude about something or someone (as illustrated in the pit-bull incident). Attitudes of greed, pride, and anger finally overflow into various forms of violence.

Attitude lies at the root of underachievement at school. Many kids don't want to, don't have to, or don't think they can, so poor performance and bad grades naturally follow.

Attitude is a major contributor to many emotional problems, including eating disorders, compulsive behaviors, and depression. The young girl or boy who is unreasonably concerned with appearance and personal attention may develop these traits. He will act out in a variety of difficult-to-correct, destructive ways. All of this begins when positive attitudes are not encouraged or when winsome outlooks are replaced with self-doubt and negativity. A recent survey indicates that nearly 45% of nine-year-olds had dieted because of parental comments and suggestions concerning their appearance. Emotional problems such as these can turn bright, young kids into truly desperate and self-destructive persons.

Attitude lies at the root of racism. Too many people falsely think their skin color makes them better than someone with a darker tone. They don't care to understand and appreciate a different culture and history. They hurt others and miss out on opportunities for a more fulfilled life experience.

Many parents focus so much on the day-to-day tasks that they pass up many valuable teaching opportunities concerning attitude. Teaching opportunities happen by sharing experiences and stories, encouraging, complimenting, and genuinely praising your children. It happens by being willing to stop and address a child's negative attitude when displayed.

When teaching positivity to children, they must have a consistent example. Without it, they can't take it seriously. When complaining, excuse-making and arguing are the norm at home, that's what's learned. They'll develop a complaining, blaming, and argumentative attitude. If prejudice is exhibited through mean and derogatory speech, a child learns to speak that way. The young person begins to believe that they're better than another group of people. They develop an attitude of superiority. And so the learning-by-bad-example goes. Conversely, when we demonstrate healthy and positive perspectives, this is what is modeled and learned.

As parents, it's our responsibility to teach the truths and realities of life. We do this so that our children will gain a proper perspective of right and wrong. Each of us, in our heart of hearts, understands these truths. We've been there. We've experienced the pleasure and pain of our decisions, which has made us aware of what is right and what is wrong. We all know that we shouldn't gossip, complain, cheat, steal, demean, or manipulate. We all know that we should learn to exhibit self-control and foster kindness, honesty, graciousness, devotion, virtue, and selflessness. We have the ability within us to extend the healthy perspectives on life for the development of a genuinely positive attitude. Healthy perspectives affect our children's overall attitudes, which come to the forefront as they face the multitude of life's challenges.

Millions of people live lives contrary to what they know in their heart is right and best for the soul. Turmoil, the direct result of their own poor decisions, surrounds them. It's nearly impossible for these people to significantly teach the principles, the Fair Warnings if they haven't yet begun to master the principles themselves. Instead, they present a confusing, contradictory perspective to the child. When teaching a young boy to control his temper after an angry outburst, mom or dad must possess the self-discipline required to manage their own angry outbursts. Thus, parents must present a consistent perspective of the principle so children will learn by example.

For those who seem or feel trapped by their shortcomings, I recall the notion of a paradigm shift, as explained by Dr. Stephen R. Covey in *Principle-Centered Leadership*. He describes a paradigm as "...your scheme for understanding and explaining certain aspects of reality." A paradigm shift then is a change in the explanation and understanding or a breakthrough in one's approach toward friends, family, decision-making, etc. In other words, "...breaks with old ways of thinking."

Some of your flaws may not seem too significant. Or you might not see any real reason to change. A more in-depth, honest look may reveal a new angle, an entirely new way of thinking. You might ask yourself: What are my weaknesses? How will my flaws affect my children? My spouse? How much better could I be if I took control of my shortcomings? What might be the result if I get professional help for a detrimental, life-long habit? These probing questions and input from loved ones may spark the needed shift of perspective or paradigm shift spurring you into action. This is the kind of work that can cause immediate positive changes, preparing you for more significant influence and respect within your home.

In Bowling Green, Ohio, student Robert Ricketts, 19, had his head bloodied when he was struck by a Conrail train. He told police he was trying to see how close to the moving train he could place his head without getting hit.

I use this ridiculous story to point out that we act just as foolishly as Robert when we continue to behave in ways which have proven ineffective time and time again. It might be time for a tremendous personal paradigm shift.

However, this undertaking isn't easy. The willingness to make sacrifices and shed weaknesses in the form of bad habits and unhealthy perspectives is a lifelong effort. The results derived from such pursuits benefit so many beyond oneself; parents, siblings, spouse, children, and co-workers all benefit. It's worth the effort.

When we commit to making our lives better, we are most effective at teaching our children what it means for them. With the added value of example, you more effectively teach them that paying the price for a disciplined mind, disciplined behavior, and a positive attitude can pave the way for greatness from any set of circumstances. That understanding will carry them through all of life's obstacles to the realization of their ambitions.

I'm trying to raise my children with a correct perspective of right and wrong so that they will have the best outlook and attitude when faced with their critical decisions in life. If successful, they'll have an attitude of healthy optimism, which will help them refuse to be involved in the activities and behaviors they've learned are detrimental to them. And when difficulties and obstacles come their way, they'll have the attitude needed to see the good in every circumstance.

This quality of optimism or positive attitude is illustrated nicely in this little story found in *More Sower's Seeds* about twin brothers. One a complaining pessimist. The other, a forever optimist:

>*Concerned about their differences, the parents decide to take their boys to a local psychologist.*
>
>*After several evaluations, the psychologist suggests a plan to balance the twin's personalities. "On their next birthday," he advises, "put them in separate rooms to open their gifts. Give the pessimist the best toys you can afford, and give the optimist a box of manure." The parents follow the instructions and carefully observe the results.*
>
>*The parents watch as the pessimist eagerly opens his present. Inside he found a new computer and a great new video game. Immediately, the little boy says aloud, "This is the OLD computer! And I don't even like this game; I know someone who has a much nicer computer than this."*
>
>*Disappointed, the parents meander down the hall to watch the second little boy open his present. They peek inside his room and find the little boy gleefully digging through the box of manure and throwing it up in the air. Giggling, he says, "You can't fool me! Where there's this much manure, there's gotta be a pony!"*

Maybe this boy was a little disillusioned in his optimism, but I think he'll go places in the years to come. With an attitude like that, there will be little chance of changing his perspective and steering him away from his goals and decisions to do the right things.

This *Fair Warning* of a positive attitude is crucial. It will affect every aspect of a person's life. Your children will begin to cultivate a mindset that will help them through life's inevitable tragedies, but more practically, they'll know how to maneuver through life's daily challenges effectively.

CHAPTER 7:
Hard Work, Honesty, and the Truth about Money

Work is honorable. It is good therapy for most problems. It is the antidote for worry. Work makes it possible for the average to approach genius. When work and duty and joy are commingled, then man is at his best.
—J. Richard Clarke

This is rather hard to admit, but as a kid, I was unusually resistant to work or, perhaps I should say, to hard labor. I know, most kids don't beg to go out and bundle branches, pull weeds, and get the yard cleaned up. But most kids don't cry about it either when they are 14 years old. I did. And I don't mean whine. I mean, really crying, unable to catch my breath crying. Blubbering. I ended up having to do the work, but with tear-stained eyes and slobbery sleeves. None of my friends ever knew of my extended years of childlike wailing. It was one of our family secrets—a Chavez family skeleton.

Part of this emotional problem was due to the trauma sustained while temporarily employed by family friends. You see, not only did I resist working initially, but once I began, it became evident that I wasn't all that efficient.

On one occasion, while working for our good friend, Dave, I was given a simple, singular assignment. Dave was clearing avocado trees from his lot with a backhoe. Another worker was cutting all the branches into small pieces. My job was to bundle, drag, and throw the debris into the large trash bin.

Everything was going just fine for a couple of hours, and at that point that my mind began to wander a little. I was now throwing the sticks into the bin, one at a time, imagining that I was pitching strikes and throwing martial arts weaponry. I abandoned the bundling technique. I thought I was doing the job too quickly and was afraid Dave would tell me to do something else, like dig a trench. So, I lollygagged a bit. (This is part of the efficiency deficit alluded to earlier.)

After finding one particularly gnarly, knotted branch, I quickly whipped around and winged it toward the bin. This branch was in a C-shape, and it sort of hooked off my hand and veered off to the right, just missing the container and squarely hitting our friend, John, in the forehead. He collapsed like a wet noodle as blood oozed out of the gash.

John survived after receiving a few stitches. Dave lost about $600 that day, thanks to me. That was the last time I was asked to work on that job-site.

On another occasion, I was babysitting two brothers, about 7 and 9 years old. The parents told me they would play nicely outside, and I would just have to watch them.

The parents had been gone for only 20 minutes when I decided to go inside to make a quick phone call. I needed to arrange a ride to the beach for the following morning—obviously, a very urgent and justified phone call. Within minutes, I heard a terrible shriek of pain in the front yard. In ran the younger boy, followed by his guilty-looking big brother. The little boy was holding his arm, crying and screaming, "I hurt my arm! I hurt my arm!" I asked if I could see, and he held out his little limb. As soon as he held it out, it swooped down and bent as if he had a new joint between his wrist and elbow. My blood ran cold; I thought I would vomit.

After scrambling to find a way over to the hospital, I sat in the emergency room for about five hours, waiting for his mother and father to arrive. My anxiety about explaining the event to them was compounded by the sad yelping and crying that continued as the medical staff worked to set his little bones. When his mom and dad finally arrived, they were gracious and understanding. So much so that they asked if I could watch the boys the next weekend. I declined. I officially retired from all employment on that day.

However, while in retirement, thankfully, my mom provided a situation that forced me to continue to learn the value of work and responsibility.

Soon after I turned 12, my mom called me to come down to the laundry room. She handed me a detergent box, threw a load of my dirty clothes onto the washer, and abruptly announced, "You are now going to do your laundry!"

Curiously I asked, "Oh, you mean...today?"

"No," she said, "Forever!" Without allowing me to begin my certain tirade of complaints, she said, "Divide your clothes into piles of whites, darks, and everything in between. Throw them in the washer separately, along with one scoop of detergent. Then, you just turn the knob to this line, close the door, and push start. When it's done, put everything in the dryer, close the door, turn the knob to 'High,' and hit 'Start.'"

I squeaked in, "But, I..." Quickly she interrupted, "And be sure to get them out of the dryer soon or they'll be wrinkled. Don't mix any colors with your whites. Plan on losing socks." She left the room, and I was a changed boy.

I quickly realized that this was one chore I could not avoid. Wearing dirty clothes was simply not acceptable. Even young kids do not appreciate the stench of dirty, wrinkled clothes. I tried to disguise the odor with Jean Nate roll-on deodorant, but it just didn't work. I was losing friends and losing them fast. I had to adjust my attitude and get the job done.

Eventually, I restored old friendships but ended up with a closet full of wrinkled, pink church shirts, and a drawer full of pink underwear. I rarely wore a set of matching socks throughout that school year, but I was slowly learning to work.

At 15 or 16, I finally snapped out of it. I got a job as a dishwasher and then a busboy. I ran the early shift at the local donut store, served frozen yogurt with a smile at Checkers, and drove a wholesale flower company's delivery route.

Work was required, and I was beginning to understand the value of it. Now responsible for specific tasks, I began to recognize the benefit of honesty. I began to realize that our character gets tested nearly every day we work for a day's wage.

The issue of honesty seems to surface very early. Who teaches kids to fib? I don't know who does initially, but children sure become aware of this tactic early on.

Case in point—between my 5th and 6th years, while supposedly taking a nap, I crept into the hallway while my mother was in the other room packing boxes for our move. I came across my mom's purse sitting on a chair. For whatever reason, I opened her wallet, took out all the bills, and stashed them away.

With the goods hidden, I denied any involvement when asked if I knew anything about the missing money. The mystery continued for two or three days, and I began to grasp the seriousness when I overheard my parents discussing "hundreds of dollars."

Finally, to pull it off, I decided to show my big brother some money that I, "...found over at the park. I was digging under the play spaceship and found it in the sand." I casually told him, "You can have it if you want."

I did the best I could to get rid of the evidence, but I had a pretty strong case stacked against me. I would never have guessed that my brother Chris was an informant.

Young kids do dumb things and are continually placing themselves in positions to learn. Unfortunately, too many parents don't take advantage of these glaring opportunities. They don't sit down and talk to their children about the value and necessity of honesty.

The indiscretions of youth can be laughable. Left uncorrected, though, they can become dangerous as our responsibilities increase. This truth manifested itself recently in my business.

I was glad to hire Todd. He was ambitious and a self-proclaimed religious man. He was a great salesperson and seemed to have a consistent work ethic. As he continued working with me, we became friends, and I trusted him.

About 18 months after he began, there was an incident that caused me to question his integrity. I looked into the matter and became aware of a scheme he had masterminded. Todd was stealing from us. Once we were sure what was happening, I confronted him. He flatly denied any involvement. He claimed to be innocent despite our multiple eyewitness sources and various documents and continued his denial even after he was fired.

Todd's act of dishonesty left him unemployed with no time to prepare or plan for his future. He's lucky he didn't end up in jail. He might not have lost his job had he confessed and faced up to the charges. He added insult to injury by compounding his dishonesty through denial.

Who knows when the problem began for him! He probably succeeded in similar cases of dishonesty and irresponsibility for many years. Now, his behavior had grown into a serious problem as a young father. As is almost always the case, his acts of dishonesty finally found their way to the surface. Eventually, the dishonest person forgets to cover tracks along the way, forgets who's been told what, and finally gets caught.

In another example, Scott, a very close family friend, decided to accept the Monster Burrito Challenge at a local Mexican restaurant. The challenge was for one person to eat an 8-lb. concoction of beans, sour cream, guacamole, chilies, beef, and jalapenos within one hour. The reward for meeting the challenge was a crisp $100 bill.

As the hour ended, you could see the whites of his eyes had turned bean brown. He was ill and fighting regurgitation with every mouthful. Furthermore, he was not even close to finishing the Monster.

The burrito consisted of dried out, left-over re-fried beans, dangerously hot chilies, and way too much sour cream of indeterminate origin. Thus, Scott believed that he'd been duped into eating a burrito with no appealing palatable qualities whatsoever. As he sat in the hot sun with only a small glass of water to quench his thirst, he became convinced his failure was the restaurant's plan.

Feeling justified and still determined to win, Scott began to break off large chunks of the Monster Burrito and throw them up on the patio cover next to him. After discarding enough of the burrito to finish the remainder on his own, a small crowd of customers and employees gathered around to witness the so-called accomplishment.

Suddenly, there was an awful ruckus on top of the patio cover.

Some seagulls had spotted the remains of the burrito laid out just above Scott's table. Now in a feeding frenzy, ten or more seagulls swarmed and swooped about scavenging what Scott had tossed up there. With great ferocity, the seagulls fought over these remains, causing a terrible commotion.

Bits of tortilla and beans scattered about, some even falling back onto Scott's table. It was apparent to all that the burrito fragments bore an uncanny resemblance to the Monster Burrito.

Scott lost out on being the first to conquer the Monster. He left with nothing more than an upset stomach and the request, "...please don't come back."

Scott is a noble person. That day though, probably brought on by bean overload, he suffered a brief lapse of judgment. And he was reminded that deceit makes itself known in the end.

A young person needs to understand that dishonesty will never bring the results he/she seeks. Moreover, we all must learn that we need to work hard for what we want in life. Combining a strict and unwavering attitude toward honesty with hard work, we will be valued and successful in all that we do; adding to that, a sound understanding of money leads to the creation of very wise and wealthy individuals.

The sound understanding about money I refer to is not complicated. It's the basic understanding that nothing is free. It's the realization that you must work hard for everything you want. It's a realization that material wealth alone does not constitute success. It's a basic understanding that greed, envy, and jealousy toward others' possessions are unhealthy and detrimental to your ability to build your financial foundation.

If our old employee, Todd, had had a good understanding of money, he might not have felt the desire to get ahead through a deceitful short-cut. If more children of my generation and the generation before us had learned more about character and honesty, we might have more self-sustaining Americans and far fewer crowding our jails. So many men and women are convicted of crimes directly tied to dishonesty and financial short-cuts.

It's necessary to understand these concepts as early as possible so they may take root and become what a person stands for. Without these deep convictions, one may find oneself in a critical moment of compromise that can become a terrible turning point in an otherwise accomplished life.

Sometimes, this occurs in a moment of stress or desperation when the severe trials of life are upon us. Phillips Brooks once said, "Someday, in the years to come, you will be wrestling with the great temptation, or trembling under the great sorrow of your life. But the real struggle is here, now. Now it is being decided whether, in the day of your supreme sorrow or great temptation, you shall miserably fail or gloriously conquer. Character cannot be made except by a steady, long, continuous process."

Those of us in Southern California recall the Orange County bankruptcy of 1995. Over a billion dollars was lost, $1.64 billion to be exact, through a risky, dishonest, misleading investments overseen by the former treasurer, Robert Citron. Before these events, the treasurer had what appeared to be an accomplished life and career. But it seemed the most basic forms of pride, greed, and dishonesty grew into an overwhelming financial debacle that could not be overcome. On April 27, 1995, he pled guilty to six charges of felonies and, in November of 1996, was sentenced to one year in prison along with a $100,000 fine.

At that critical moment of decision, when the treasurer allowed any degree of deception, he failed his test of character, and the results were far-reaching. So far-reaching that Citron later wrote, "After I resigned and after the bankruptcy, I contemplated suicide." Upon sentencing, Superior Court Judge J. Stephen Czuleger said concerning this former official, "He put himself in this position. He chose to engage in the type of activity over the years that he did. It caught up with him. It overcame him. And it ultimately came close to destroying him."

I believe that parents can help their children be firm in their commitment to these critical principles before they face compromising situations. Some parents do well in teaching their kids to work hard and be honest. However, they altogether neglect to teach them anything about the nature of money and how it can create wealth or ruin.

Consider the ease of credit card use. As soon as a person earns wages, the enticement is to "buy now, pay later," all with the swipe of a card. As we all know, millions go overboard and quickly find themselves in a deep financial bind.

Why not take some time to explain the basics of the financial system before sending children off to college? Why not set up a savings program for them, to which they can contribute? Why not loan them a little money with interest, and teach them what happens when they overextend themselves?

Financial conflict is one of the most significant factors contributing to divorce. Erratic spending habits, mismanagement, greed, and dishonesty cause of some horrible arguments. Disputes like these strike at the foundation of a marriage and a family.

Kids deserve a *Fair Warning* about these things. And the sooner, the better. In October 1994, *Reader's Digest* featured an article entitled "*Cheating in Our Schools: A National Scandal.*"

This article revealed an alarming attitude of American youth. "Honesty and integrity have been replaced in many classrooms by a win-at-any-cost attitude that puts grades, expediency, and personal gain above all else. 'Moral standards have become so eroded that many children can no longer tell right from wrong,' says Kevin Ryan, founding director of the Center for the Advancement of Ethics and Character at Boston University."

In the article, educational psychologist, Fred Schab shared his 1969 and 1989 surveys of high school students. In 1969, 34% admitted cheating on tests; by 1989, that figure had doubled. In 1969, 58% of students let other students copy their homework; by 1989, 98% said they had.

One student commented, "Cheating has become a guiltless type of thing. Ten minutes of cheating is better than two hours studying." When one teacher was asked why he tolerated such widespread cheating, he gave this shocking reply, "If we stopped our students from cheating, they would be at a competitive disadvantage."

The article concludes with these words of wisdom from Al Burr, a former public high school principal, "We need to focus on producing young adults who know how to behave when nobody's watching." Jay Mulkey, president of the non-profit Character Education Institute in San Antonio, TX, states, "Cheating is habit-forming. Students who cheat in class may well cheat in their jobs or on their spouses. When you have a country that doesn't value honesty and thinks that character is unimportant, what kind of society do you have?"

Show your children how to work. Teach them the value of rigorous honesty. Share with them your experiences about the dangerous disillusionments associated with money.

If you never see your teenager studying, and he/she brings home a 3.5 GPA, please don't flatter yourself. He or she may have learned the convenience of cheating. It is up to you, the parent, to teach your children why they shouldn't.

I had a friend who brought home a 3.5 GPA that way. He attended one of the prestigious University of California campuses. His parents were very proud. When he arrived on campus, he had no idea what he was doing. After one year, he had flunked entirely. For the time being, he is another statistic among the complacent segment of Generation X.

Teach the next generation the values of hard work, honesty, and the truth about money. Let them know they may not get everything they want when they want it. Although they may have to forego some of the immediate pleasures, they'll have the lasting benefits of personal satisfaction that accompanies real achievement. With time and honesty, their odds for occupational security and valuable net worth will be tremendous.

CHAPTER 8:
Media

Nearly all parents want to convey to their children the importance of self-discipline, hard work, and decent manners, but the entertainment media celebrate vulgar behavior, contempt for all authority, and obscene language, inserted even in 'family fare' where it is least expected.
—*Michael Medved*

FATHER'S DAY IN TELEVISION LAND, 1957:

Bud has a problem. His coach just cut him from the team. He goes to his wise, calm, and wonderful father, who offers him some sage advice, such as "Try, try again." Bud realizes that father indeed knows best. He follows pop's advice and becomes the star of the team.

FATHER'S DAY IN TELEVISION LAND, 1997:

Bart has a problem. In fact, Bart is a problem. He seeks advice from anyone and everyone but Homer, since dad doesn't know a darn thing. This is confirmed when Homer finally offers Bart direction, based on his own life views. "If something is too hard, give it up. The moral, my boy, is to never try anything."
(Paula Hunker, The Washington Times)

In many ways, the media, radio, movies, magazines, and the Internet have become the guardians of American youth. The ease by which the media is accessed and enjoyed makes for a dangerously simple way to occupy time and for parents to find a little relief from demanding children.

Media can be educational and instructional and can provide healthy entertainment. But as in all things, overexposure without oversight can lead to problems.

Consider the severe repercussions of the following example. I was in fifth or sixth grade when I walked into Jason's house after school and heard his older brothers laughing and snickering in the living room. "Hey, you guys; come in here and look at this!" We walked over, and my eyes must have been as wide as silver dollars when I saw what had the undivided attention of the four or five older boys in the room.

Their dad left a stack of hard-core porn videos behind the TV. And these boys had seen them all. Also, there was a two-foot stack of *Playboy* magazines on a bookshelf, sitting in plain view.

In retrospect, it's no wonder that by the eighth grade, Jason was having lots of sex at home before his parents came home from work. During high school, his girlfriend had her first abortion.

A recent report indicated that 76% of adults think that individual behavior is the overriding factor that contributes to many of the current problems we face in society. Ironically, of those respondents, only 11% felt that their conduct had had any adverse effect on society. Of course, it's always somebody else. I would wager that Jason's parents don't feel they're part of the problem either. In my opinion, any parent who makes little or no effort to regulate the use and consumption of media within the home is a significant part of the problem.

A 1991 survey taken by Mellman and Lazarus, "*American Family Values Study: A Return to Family Values,*" reveals that only 2% of respondents think that television *should* have the most influence on their children's values, but 56% believe it does have the most significant impact—more than parents, teachers, and religious leaders combined. Can this be true? Is the media affecting and influencing America's youth to such a degree?

In search of answers to these questions, I found rather stunning statistics, some of which may be common knowledge, and some may not.

The following information comes from an excellent talk entitled, *"Ancient and Modern Idolatry,"* given by Randal A. Wright, PhD, at the educational CES Symposium held at Brigham Young University in 1995. Wright has spent over 20 years researching the effect of the media on the family.

In Dr. Wright's talk, he shares statistics from a 1994 article featured in *USA Today.* "The report indicates that 1,490 hours were spent each year watching TV, or 4 hours each day; 1,380 hours were spent listening to radio, music, and CDs, or 3.7 hours each day; 46 hours, or about 1 hour each week, was spent at the movie theater or watching videos. Thus, the average American places himself or herself under the direct influence of the media for 2,916 hours a year or 56 hours each week! The article also notes that by the time the average American child reaches age 6, he or she has already spent more time watching TV than they will spend talking to their father in his/her entire lifetime. Do the media influence us? Can the media have more influence than parents, teachers, and religious leaders combined? I think so."

Mr. Wright quoted Spencer Kimball, who said, "Man is naturally a religious being. His heart instinctively seeks for God. Whether he reverences the sacred cow or prays to the sun or the moon; whether he kneels before wood or stone images or prays in secret to his Father in Heaven, he is satisfying an inborn urge to look to someone bigger than us." Wright proceeded to explain that the media marketers play on that truth. "They have mastered the art of capturing our attention and sounding their message in our ears. They have set up heroes for our viewing pleasure, and we gladly worship."

In one of his books, *Why Do Good People See Bad Movies?* Dr. Wright shares the findings of Dorthy Barclay, who documented startling differences in the heroes of society between

1900 and 1950. In 1900, the participants listed their heroes as follows:

> *78% historical figures*
> *12% literary figures*
> *10% relatives*

In 1950, a new element had arrived on the scene, and a dramatic change took place in less than a lifetime. The results follow:

> *33% historical figures*
> *0% literary figures*
> *10% relatives*
> *57% movie, TV, music, and sports stars*
> (Dorthy Barclay, Youth's Heroes and Hero Worship, [The New York Times Magazine], Nov. 1951, pp.42)

Dr. Wright provided some incredibly insightful statistics from his extensive survey of American youth concerning media consumption and its effects. One of several questions asked was, "If you could trade places with any individual, who would it be?" The results? Seventeen of the top 20 named were TV and movie personalities. The second largest group mentioned came from the music industry. The third-largest group named figures in the world of professional sports. Wright continues, "Aside from these studies, how do we know how much these people are admired? Look at the money we pay them to entertain us."

Citing an article published in *USA Today*, May 1993, Dr. Wright illustrated, "in 1982, the starting salary for the average American worker was $21,077. In 1991, that salary had risen to $29,421. By comparison, in 1982, the average professional basketball player earned a salary of $235,000, and by 1991, that salary had increased to $1,410,000. And this was before they got paid the big bucks!

"Here are the highest-paid athletes of 1996, as estimated by Forbes in their Dec. 16, 1996 issue (in millions):

1. Mike Tyson $75
2. Michael Jordan $52.6
3. Michael Schumacher $33
4. Shaquille O'Neal $24.4
5. Emmitt Smith $16.5
6. Evander Holyfield $15.5
7. Andre Agassi $15.2
8. Arnold Palmer $15.1
9. Dennis Rodman $12.9
10. Patrick Ewing $12.4

"When Tiger Woods announced his entrance into the world of professional golf with his historic greeting, 'Hello world,' he was enthusiastically welcomed with endorsements estimated at more than $60 million. Why such revenue? Because we are willing to pay the price. The income is proof of the influence.

"When Michael Jordan came out of college, he signed a deal with Nike worth $5 million over five years. Within those five years, sales at Nike increased by 388%. When it was rumored that Jordan might come back from retirement, *USA Today* ran this headline, "The 2 Billion Dollar Rumor." The stock of those companies he represents earned $2.3 billion over three days based solely on the rumor that he might return. Influence? I would say so."

More from Randal Wright, "ET ate a piece of candy. What was it? *Reese's Pieces*—and sales—their *(Reece's Pieces')* sales increased by 78% the next month. In 1985, the number of young men who applied to be navy fighter pilots increased dramatically. Did the movie *Top Gun* have anything to do with it? In 1993, for some strange reason, the number of people who visited and donated funds to dinosaur museums skyrocketed. *Jurassic Park*? Maybe. *Barney*? Maybe." Yes, we're influenced!

Now, what happens when one of these heroes decides to glamorize alcohol, drugs, and promiscuity? What happens when one of them acts disrespectful and rude? What's the message when Roberto Alomar spits in an umpire's face in front of millions of onlookers? What's the message when Dennis Rodman head-butts a referee and kicks a photographer? What's the message when Christian Slater, Charlie Sheen, Robert Downey Jr., and a host of others in the spotlight are hauled off to jail? What are young people learning from the likes of Marilyn Manson, who openly preaches Satanism through his music and interviews?

And what of TV and movie content? Can children be influenced heavily by it? Again, we only need to look at the dollar signs. Today, the stars of sitcoms can earn between $50 thousand and $1 million per episode. We pay the fees as we watch with ever-increasing frequency. Proof that we are heavily influenced.

In his book, *The Index of Leading Cultural Indicators*, William Bennett reminds us of a study performed by *USA Today*. In this study, *USA Today* staff members watched one week of prime-time television on ABC, NBC, CBS, and FOX. Among the findings were the following:

- Of the 45 sex scenes shown on network television, 23 were between unmarried heterosexual couples, 16 were adulterous, 4 were between married heterosexuals and 1 involved teens.

- Among the 94 shows watched, 48 showed at least one violent act. All told there were 276 acts of violence in which 57 people were killed, and 99 people were assaulted.

- Although 60% of Americans "never doubt the existence of God" and 42% attend church once a week, only 5% of TV characters practice any religion in any form.

Music also wields unique power. Plato once said, "Musical training is a more potent instrument than any other because rhythm and harmony find their way into the inward places of the soul, on which they mightily fasten, imparting grace."

In his book, Mr. Bennett tackled the impact of music on youth, including some intriguing statistics about music consumption and content:

- Fifteen- to nineteen-year-olds buy more music than any other monitored age group.

- Between the seventh and twelfth grades, the average teenager listens to 10,500 hours of rock music, just slightly less than the entire number of hours spent in the classroom from kindergarten through high school.

- In one popular album, which sold 1.7 million copies, there were 226 uses of the f-word, 81 uses of the s-word, 163 uses of the b-word, 87 descriptions of oral sex, and 117 explicit terms for male or female genitalia. *(The Index of Leading Cultural Indicators, [Touchstone; New York, 1994] pp. 104-112)*

If our children find their heroes in the media, then, overwhelmingly, these are the messages that you should expect them to receive. Yes, there are some people in professional sports and in the entertainment industries who set stellar examples. We know who they are because they stand apart from the rest, but they usually don't get quite as much attention as the ones who peddle trash. And we all know which athletes and stars peddle garbage, yet unfortunately, they are some of the most famous people in their fields.

Hero-Worship: defined in the dictionary as the "idealization of an admired man or woman" (Readers Digest Oxford, 1996). Hero: defined in the dictionary as "a person noted or admired for nobility, courage, and outstanding achievements." (ibid.) I'm afraid people have forgotten that a hero is a person who represents goodness, nobility, courage, and outstanding achievement. I'm afraid that many less-than-heroic people are idealized as heroes in this clever world of mass-marketing.

We know that to worship someone or some message takes sacrifice. We give up time, money, and effort as a faithful follower or one who worships. If this is true, the facts and figures of time and money spent on every media source by America make us a nation of media worshippers. It is a frightening thought.

We know that the media's powers specifically target young people who will make up the next generation of media consumers. In *George Magazine*, Jonathan Bernstein asked, "Does anyone these days launch a big-budget movie, album, television show, or software without factoring teen appeal into the equation? Doubtful. The kids have the disposable income, they've got the free time, and they've got the obsessive nature."

Jon Nesvig, president of the advertising for FOX, was blunt when he said, "We're selling the next generation of customers." And at FOX, they keep the next generation's attention by airing the dysfunctional likes of Married *with* Children (the longest-running sitcom on television.)

In one episode of this show, as written about in the May 1996 issue of *Reader's Digest*, the father and son rhapsodize about an upcoming trip to "the nudie bar, where you see their butt and their trap stays shut." And apparently, parents aren't turning the TV off even though this garbage is repeated each night on every major network. As one critic noted recently, "do it" is a more common television expression than "stay tuned."

Merely viewing and listening to the dangerous depictions and innuendos may seem harmless to some parents. "Oh, my kids won't go off and do all that," may be the rationalization. Maybe they won't. But they'll never really know their children's weaknesses and proclivities until they rear their ugly heads.

Regarding "merely viewing and listening," these parents either forget or fail to realize that, as expressed by Mr. Simon Winchester, "...such things can only tempt those who verge on such acts to take a greater interest in them."

The facts are clear. Media has an overwhelming impact on children, teens, and the entire society. What then will you do about it? How much will you allow? Will you extend a Fair Warning to your children about the harmful effects of the media? Are you willing to take the time to seek out the healthy, value-oriented programming? Are you ready to help your kids accurately judge what they view?

I share these points and statistics to illustrate how much these mediums are being consumed and how much detrimental information is out there. What then will you do about it? How much of it will you allow in your home? Will you extend a Fair Warning to your children about the adverse effects of the media? Are you willing to take the time to seek out the healthy, value-oriented programming that's out there? Are you ready to help your kids wisely judge what they consume?

While growing up, most of my friends had no restrictions. The use of TV and media was an entertainment free-for-all. Overconsumption dulls the senses. It encourages laziness, compromises judgment, and invites trouble. We are now witnessing this within large segments of my generation.

A severe dulling of the senses occurred in the life of Jeremy Strohmeyer, 18, of Long Beach, Calif. Strohmeyer allegedly raped and strangled seven-year-old Sherice Iverson, while vacationing in a Primm, NV casino.

In June 1997, *People Magazine* reported, "Little in Strohmeyer's apparently ordinary, middle-class background—his mother, Winifred, is a marketing executive; his father, John, a well-to-do real estate investor—seems to account for the callousness of the murder of which he is accused." But a more in-depth look reveals a bit more. Jeremy had recently dropped out of athletics, and his grades dropped dramatically. He was suspected of using methamphetamines and was kicked out of his house for repetitive curfew violations. And there was another hint of a darker side. A friend, Andy Edling, says that earlier this year, Strohmeyer had shown him an extensive collection of pornographic photos culled from the Internet. 'What struck me most was the little children,' Edling says. 'I thought it was gross, and he just laughed.'" This frightening scenario begs the questions: How much media was he allowed to access over the years? How much impact did this consumption of Internet smut have on his apparent decision to commit such an act?

Eugene L. Roberts, a great teacher and coach, wrote of a life-changing event during adolescence. While growing up, he had drifted aimlessly with the wrong kind of friends. One night while hanging around, Eugene saw a large group entering the local tabernacle. He had nothing better to do, so he wandered in. He met up with some friends, and they settled next to a group of girls who seemed to promise some amusement. They had no interest in the message coming from the pulpit and immediately began with their disruptive antics. Right amid their disturbance, he writes, "There thundered from the pulpit the following statement: 'You can't tell the character of an individual by the way he does his daily work. Watch him when his work is done. See where he goes. Note the companions he seeks and the things he does when he may do as he pleases. Then you can tell his true character.' I looked up toward the rostrum," Roberts continues, "because I was struck with this powerful statement.

"The speaker went on to make this comparison. He said, 'Let us take the eagle, for example. This bird works as hard and as efficiently as any other animal or bird in doing its daily work. It provides for itself and its young by the sweat of its brow, so to speak, but when its daily work is over and the eagle has time to do as it pleases, note how it spends its recreational moments. It flies in the highest realms of heaven, spreads its wings and bathes in the upper air, for it loves the pure, clean atmosphere and the lofty heights.

"'On the other hand, let us consider the hog. This animal grunts and grubs and provides for its young just as well as the eagle; but when its working hours are over and it has some recreational moments, observe where it goes and what it does. The hog will seek out the muddiest hole in the pasture and will roll and soak itself in filth, for this is the thing it loves. People can be either eagles or hogs in their leisure time.'

"Now when I heard this short speech," writes Gene Roberts, "I was dumbfounded. I turned to my companions abashed, for I was ashamed to be caught listening. What was my surprise to find every one of the gang with his attention fixed upon the speaker and his eyes containing a far-away expression.

"We went out of the tabernacle that evening rather quiet and we separated from each other unusually early. I thought of that speech all the way home. I classified myself immediately as of the hog family. I thought of that speech for years. That night there was implanted within me the faintest beginnings of ambition to lift myself out of the hog group and to rise to that of the eagle.

"There was instilled in me that evening, the urge to help fill up the mud holes in the social pasture so that those people with hog tendencies would find it difficult to wallow in recreational filth. As a result of constantly thinking about that speech, I was stirred to devote my whole life and profession toward developing wholesome recreational activities for the young people, so that it would be natural and easy for them to indulge in the eagle-type of leisure." *(Raymond Brimhall Holbrook & Esther Hamilton Holbrook, The Tall Pine Tree, 1988, pp. 111–113)*

Two points are working here. The first is that this man was changed forever because of one good message. He was in the right place at the right time and heard a message that stirred him to wake up and change. If the average time spent consuming media can be cut in half, or even by one quarter, a better activity or message can replace it. That better use of time might change a life forever.

The second point is one of character. What kind of human beings do you want to raise? Will you allow your kids to wallow in the mire as the dirty, old hog, or will you inspire them to maximize their potential and soar like an eagle? Kids deserve to learn that the way they spend their own time affects who they become and what they represent.

What you've read here isn't a commentary against all forms of leisure via media. We all have our favorite athletes. We have our music and our shows. But we can moderate and choose wisely.

My children won't be sheltered from all modern media; they shouldn't be. But what they watch, and how often they watch it will be monitored. There will be no confusion about who their heroes are. I don't want my children to, as William Bennett phrased it, to "confuse fame with importance." Children will benefit in various ways if parents actively seek out and present their children with many true heroes to emulate.

The wise Sir Gallahad once proclaimed, "My strength is as the strength of ten because my heart is pure!" His heart was pure because his mind was free from the world's impurities. He used his leisure time in the most uplifting ways and became a man of significant influence.

I recently read a comic strip by John McPherson depicting two mechanics talking with a customer. The first mechanic said to the patron, "Wade here thinks it's your distributor, but I happen to think it's your carburetor. So, we made a compromise and changed your water pump." Don't compromise your child's future by expecting someone else to do what's best for them.

There is no question that all of us, and especially our children, are persuaded continuously by every form of modern media. We can enjoy what is worthwhile and enlightening in the media. We can learn from that which is educational. Let's follow our favorite teams, rent good movies, and buy uplifting CDs. But we need to rise above the smut. Shun the baseless garbage. Find out what your kids are listening to, what they're watching, and what they're reading. One day they'll thank you.

CHAPTER 9:
The Party Scene

Even now, when the dangers of drug abuse are well understood, many educated people still discuss the drug problem in almost every way except the right way. They rarely speak plainly—drug use is wrong because it is immoral, and it is immoral because it enslaves the mind and destroys the soul.
—James Q. Wilson, UCLA

One summer afternoon, I watched my friend Kevin singe his eyelashes and eyebrows entirely off. We were in the fourth grade then and were out at his backyard table where he was making a "joint," basil leaves and oregano rolled in typing paper. Lighting the end of his stogie, Kevin confidently inhaled. Once lit, it acted as a bellows, immediately engulfing the entire concoction. It burned off whatever follicles were in range while sending a harsh stream of smoke and ash down his windpipe—followed by a fit of coughing and hacking.

Innocent curiosity? Sure. I felt uneasy being there since I knew I was flirting with something I shouldn't. On the other hand, Kevin, despite his near-death experience, went on to become well-known throughout the high schools as the guy who could always "get you some weed." He didn't stop at innocent curiosity because he didn't feel like it was wrong. After all, he was only doing what his older brothers did and was allowed by their parents.

One of my best friends recalls his first curiosities about drugs. It was one night when he was about thirteen years old. He watched a then-popular movie called Go Ask Alice. The film is a portrayal of a young girl caught up in drug use. The story piqued his curiosity. He stayed curious until he found his first opportunity to experiment with drugs. That sparked the beginning of a 15-year battle.

My friend's experience was not unlike that of most people who end up with drug problems. Whether it's alcohol, nicotine, or harder drugs, most people are exposed to them in one form or another at an early age. It's not hard for a parent to think, "Not my child. He's too young. He runs around with good kids."

One well-intentioned mother I knew had a carefree attitude about her "good kids." She assumed that her two boys and two girls were too young to get into real trouble. She trusted them so much that they could come and go as they pleased, making it possible for her to work late into the evenings. Her 13-year-old daughter seemed to be a great babysitter.

The result? They had the shelter and physical supervision necessary to sustain life, and everyone got along pretty well and enjoyed a lot of good times, but that was all. They were left to learn about life without any counsel, warning, or discipline.

In junior high, that home was the official "hang-out" house. Every day before mom came home, the kids would gather to smoke marijuana, drink, and mess around in empty bedrooms. This trend continued in high school, and mom continued to arrive home just after the mess was straightened up as the last few kids were leaving. The kids would flash an innocent smile and say goodnight when she came home.

Today, all her children (now young adults) are wallowing in drug problems and are struggling to realize a successful future.

This mom wasn't wrong to think she had good kids and to trust them. And that's just it. They were great kids, each of them. But the greatest of kids left unattended and unaccountable can quickly squander their potential. Opportunity to veer off track is everywhere, and early.

The first time I was offered pot was in the sixth grade. There were kids in my junior high school who came to class drunk.

Usually, they stole alcohol from their parents' liquor cabinet before leaving the house. As a freshman, I had friends who became heavy users of cocaine and LSD.

In a recent survey of 12- to17-year-olds, over half said heroin and cocaine are very accessible. The University of Michigan's Institute for Social Research reports that daily marijuana use among eighth-graders has more than quadrupled since 1992.

Eighth Grade. That's when I faced some of those critical choices for myself. I didn't always choose wisely. It was during that time when my mom used to drop me off at the Camarillo Cinema with friends. One night, we had about an hour before our movie began.

We were all riding our skateboards through the plaza and just wasting time. I noticed a few of the guys huddling together near the alleyway in the back of the theater. I went over and saw one of the younger kids taking a drag off a "clove" cigarette. All the other boys were eagerly grabbing for the next puff. "Here, man, give it to me, give it to me!" One of them said as they all scrambled after it. "Lick your lips after you take a puff; it tastes like candy!" said someone else. Another bragged, "Oh man, my head is buzzing. Give me that thing again!" And on and on, they continued.

It was dark now, and I started to look around to see if anyone could see us. I was making sure the coast was clear as I struggled with the thought of trying it myself. They lit another one. My heart was pounding. When it finally came my way, I took it.

I had barely inhaled when I nervously looked out into the parking lot and saw two headlights driving directly towards us. We were all standing behind the trash bin, and I peered out toward the headlights. My face was caught directly in the beam of light as smoke whirled from my mouth. I recognized the truck. It was my big brother! He honked his horn and waved me over to him. All of my little cohorts scattered. "Get in the truck. I'm taking you home so you can tell mom and dad about this."

I walked upstairs to tell my dad what had happened. I was disheartened to find him lifting weights. He was wearing a white T-shirt and gray sweats. He looked like a criminal who was pumping iron in the yard. I finally found the courage to tell him why I was home early, and he took me downstairs to have "a little chat with your mother."

The three of us sat together on the couch. My mom put her arm around me as we talked about what went on. They asked me why I had gone against what they had taught me over the years. They reminded me why decisions like these are so significant. There was no yelling. There was disappointment and concern expressed lovingly.

My dad said, "So, do you want to go see the rest of that movie?"

"Really?" I asked. "Well, can I trust you or not?" he returned.

So, I went back to the movies that night, and my friends learned that those things matter in our family.

This definitely wasn't the last time I'd disappoint them. But knowing that I was making poor decisions sometimes and knowing that my parents cared about it was enough to motivate me to make course corrections.

The other boys involved that night didn't have the same motivation from their parents. They didn't have a reason to stay away from the Party Scene and went along with it. There was no such thing as a moral dilemma when faced with drugs and alcohol. One of the boys with me that night began high school as a star football player. By his sophomore year, he quit the team. Then, he dropped out of school during his junior year due to his drinking problem.

The odds are stacked against children these days. In many cases, young people's problems with alcohol and drugs can be expected, considering what they see at home. Alcohol and drugs are a normal part of life there. As parent's drink, smoke, or take drugs at home, it's usually not a question of if that child will do the same, but when.

As a teenager, my neighbors were a typical social drinking family, not unlike millions of families. They were nice people. One day, I was shooting baskets with their 16-year-old son, and out of curiosity, I asked him, "Hey, do your parents care if you drink sometimes?"

"Not really!" he said. "But I guess they would ground me if they knew I was drinking a lot before I was 21, or at least in college."

Digging a little deeper, I asked, "Do you think you'll drink much when you do get to college or turn 21?"

With a big grin, he bragged, "Right now, I just don't get caught. But you wait and see, Chavez, when I'm outta the house, I'm gonna drink like a madman!"

While it was good that his parents didn't "allow" drinking while underage, they made little attempt to suggest that he could be better off if he didn't drink. For him, alcohol was in no way discouraged, only postponed. To not drink wasn't explored.

Mark Keiman, a UCLA professor specializing in national drug policy, reminds us we should not ignore the fact that "... the No. 1 drug of abuse among high school kids: alcohol." Why then are so many parents willing to overlook the glaring risks? Forget alcoholism for a moment; why not guide kids as far away from heart and liver disease as possible? Wouldn't most parents be willing to do anything possible to protect their children from becoming another sad statistic? Aren't we willing to do anything, including giving up our unhealthy habits for the kids' sake?

I wish there were a statistic indicating how many people become alcoholics and addicts as a direct result of the influence within their home. Society spends some time addressing peer pressure, but I've never heard a real discussion about the impact of familial influences.

Harold Morris shares a story about a teenager killed in an alcohol-related car wreck. Late one evening, a police officer had the unfortunate duty of delivering the tragic news of a young boy's death to his family. When the tired father opened the door, the police officer said solemnly, "Sir, I regret to inform you that your son was killed this evening while behind the wheel." The man stood silent and stunned. He motioned for the officer to come inside, and the officer continued, "Sir, I further regret to inform you that your son was also under the influence of alcohol. This is a drunk-driving fatality."

In a sudden outburst of rage, the man slammed his fist against a barstool and said, "I swear if I ever find out who gave him something to drink, I'll kill 'em!" His agony and frustration were overwhelming. Wanting to calm his nerves, the distraught father walked behind the bar, set out a shot glass, and opened the liquor cabinet. A piece of note paper fell to the floor. He picked it up and read these words:

Dad,
Went out with the guys today, and we took a fifth of vodka.
We knew you wouldn't mind! See ya later!
Andy

While working last year, I overheard many young kids talking with a security guard. I looked over just as he sat down and took a cigar from his shirt pocket. As he lit it and took the first puff, the kids crowded around him. As one would expect, a brave, obnoxious little boy said, "Hey, let me try some of that! I've had one before, let me see it. I'll show you." The guard just chuckled a little and started to look around. He had no idea that I was watching him. "No, you better not," he said with a puff of cigar smoke. But the little guy persisted, and a few of the other kids egged him on. "Just let him try it," one girl chided. The security guard finally relented and started to hand the cigar to the boy who couldn't have been more than 9 or 10 years old.

Just then, I stepped out from beside my car and shouted, "Hey, what kind of security guard do you think you are? Keep that thing to yourself!" All heads snapped like slingshots in my direction. Some people were sitting around eating lunch and sipping coffee; everyone looked over. The young kids high-tailed it out of there and this pathetic, embarrassed man smirked and said, "Well, he did ask for it." There are far too many people willing to give your kids whatever they ask for.

It's up to you to give your kids a Fair Warning concerning these things. Help them avoid the severe consequences of this Party Scene. Rarely does anyone graduate to hardcore drug-use without having experimented with alcohol and cigarettes first. You have the power to create clear guidelines that don't allow room for rationalization or compromise in this area.

When, as in many cases, kids don't seem to end up going off the deep end, and everything seems to be just good fun, they still run the risk of developing big problems years later. They can become violent over time, get fired in their 40s, lose a family, or exacerbate emotional problems; after they have long since left your care. Parents who fail to teach and warn about these dangers or even encourage them through their bad example are not without some responsibility when the serious problems surface years later. Remember, while they may not all become drug addicts or drunks many may not be able to avoid the consequences of health problems mentioned previously.

Seriously consider making a sacrifice for your children. Isn't it worth diminishing the high risks for them, whether it be time, counseling, deeper relationships, or giving up your temporary pleasures? Wouldn't this add greater satisfaction to your own life as well as theirs?

There was once a builder hired to construct a home for a very wealthy man. "Spare no expense!" he said. "I refuse to accept anything but the very best." The builder happened to be going through some difficult times financially, so he decided to skimp. He knew that he could make the structure appear as top quality while saving thousands for himself. He would accomplish this using lower-quality material beneath the surface and take less time by eliminating quality details not noticed on the exterior.

When the job was complete, the customer complimented the contractor on what seemed to be a job well done. The builder gave him his set of keys. Then, without warning, the wealthy gentleman turned to the young builder and said, "Friend, I already have a beautiful home like this. So, as a gift, now I want to give this home to you. I hope you and your family will enjoy living in the finest home you were able to build."

The man's heart ached. He earned a few thousand dollars because he cut corners. Now he has a beautiful home, but he'll be forever reminded of what could have been. We owe it to our children and ourselves to decide not to skimp when it comes to raising our families.

Parents are the best hope in this arena. No one has more influence on your child than you. Inevitably, many will wander into the fun and seemingly harmless experiences with alcohol and drug use, which can quickly become a dark and dangerous forest—the exit from which can be very difficult to make. But you, the parent, are like no other and can lead them through the unavoidable pressures to participate. You may help them avoid getting lost in the forest altogether. Or, you may have the more difficult task of going into the woods and attempt to lead him/her back out as many families must do.

In the classic, *Les Miserables*, Victor Hugo beautifully illustrates one such rescue from one of life's forests. Hugo vividly describes this forest, used here as a metaphor for the very dark and trying times of life. The dark and trying times that people sometimes place themselves in. So dark and even terrifying that only the person experiencing it and the angels above really know. He captures the relief that comes to the sorrowing soul when the hand of a Samaritan is finally extended and received.

Hopefully, you can teach your children so that they never need to experience such a burden.

I hope the following excerpt inspires every parent to do all in his/her power to keep his/her children out of the Party Scene, which is the entryway to some of life's dangerous forests. Also, may this illustration encourage parents to go into the forest and attempt to lead them out safely.

In this scene, the eight-year-old, Cosette, is abandoned in a forest by the Thenardiess, her abusive and uncaring foster mother. She experiences fear and a burden, which she simply cannot bear alone. She longs to be rescued from this terrible place. She is finally recovered from her horror by the man who would become her father.

I cannot emphasize enough that the Party Scene is a forever-beckoning gateway to such a forest. A forest from which many cannot return on their own. A deceptively fascinating forest that thousands of kids willingly and anxiously enter. A forest so powerful and appealing that some of its travelers can never be lured out. A forest from which many who entered might have initially fled had they been carefully led away from it by consistent and involved parents.

Without being conscious of what she was experiencing, Cosette felt seized by this black enormity of nature. It was not merely terror that held her but something even more terrible. She shuddered. Words fail to express the peculiar strangeness of that shudder, which chilled her through and through.

Then, by some sort of instinct, to get out of this singular state, which she did not understand but which terrified her, she began to count aloud, one, two, three, four, up to ten, and when she had finished, she began again. This restored her to a real perception of the things around her. Her hands, which were wet from drawing water, felt cold. She stood up. Her fear had returned, a natural and insurmountable fear. She had only one thought, to flee; to flee at top speed, across woods, across fields, to the houses and windows and lighted candles. Her eyes fell on the bucket there in front of her. Such was the dread the Thenardiess inspired in her. She did not dare leave without the bucket of water. She grasped the handle with both hands. She could hardly lift it.

She went a dozen steps this way, but the bucket was full, it was heavy, she had to rest it on the ground. She caught her breath an instant, then grasped the handle again, and walked on, this time a little longer. But she had to stop again. After resting a few seconds, she started on. She walked bending forward, her head down, like an old woman; the weight of the bucket strained and stiffened her tiny arms. The iron handle was numbing and freezing her little wet hands; from time to time, she had to stop, and every time she stopped, the cold water that sloshed out of the bucket splashed onto her bare knees. This took place in the depth of the woods, at night, in the winter, far from all human sight; she was a child of eight. At that moment, only the Eternal father saw this sad thing.

And undoubtedly her mother, alas!

For there are things that open the eyes of the dead in their grave.

Her breath came as a kind of painful gasp; sobs choked her, but she did not dare weep.

She was worn out and was not yet out of the forest. Reaching an old chestnut tree, she knew, she made one last halt, longer than the others, to rest up well, then she gathered all her strength, took up her bucket again, and began walking on courageously. Meanwhile, the poor little despairing thing could not help crying: "Oh my God! Oh, God!"

At that moment, she suddenly felt the weight of the bucket was gone. A hand, which seemed enormous to her, had just caught the handle, and was carrying it easily. She looked up. A large dark form, straight and erect, was walking beside her in the darkness. A man who had come up behind her and whom she had not heard. This man, without saying a word, had grasped the handle of the bucket she was carrying.

There are instincts for all the crises of life.

The child was not afraid.

(Les Miserables *[New York: NAL Penguin, Inc., 1987], pp. 389–390.)*

CHAPTER 10:
Love and Sex

*Sex is now being made into the measure of existence, and such uniquely
human qualities as modesty, fidelity, abstinence, chastity, delicacy, and
shame, qualities that formerly provided the constraints on sexual activity
and the setting within which the erotic passion was
enjoyed are today ridiculed.*
—*Walter Berns, 1976*

While the average income in America remains quite high
and 95% of Americans remain employed, over 55%
of all marriages now end in divorce. Income levels and employment rates remain steady because we continue to produce
willing workers with sufficient knowledge to sustain the system. We send our kids to college and try to teach them to work
hard, making a specific effort to see our children succeed in
this area.

On the other hand, divorce rates soar because many young
people may not have realized that successful relationships require more effort than holding down a steady job.

Today, kids are mainly left to themselves to figure out the
complexities of love, relationships, and sex. We do relatively
little to guide them toward successful marriages and parenting.
A college education, a good job, and a stable income don't
mean much when you're all alone. And there are very few who
want to live life alone. A recent survey in the Orange County
Register indicates that 80% of men and 88% of women want
to marry and raise a family someday.

There are scores of men and women throughout the world
who are highly intelligent and excel in the workplace, yet can't

tionlan quArationquantation

seem to find the same consistency and happiness in their personal lives where they yearn for it most. Their career growth and success is evidence that they possess the ability to succeed at home as well. But for whatever reasons, they are not living up to that potential.

These professionals earned their skills and knowledge through rigorous study and dedication. They secured steady jobs and advancement because of their hard work, collaboration, and ability to learn new skills.

Why then, do so many of these talented people fall short of their desires in their relationships? Why all of the divorces? Why all of the running around? Why all of the arguments? Because so many of them were never given any training, guidance, or encouragement in this area. They were left to figure it all out on their own through trial and error. And when applying that method of learning, there will be many serious errors made.

My friend, Aaron, at 23 years has already faced significant problems in his young love life. He fathered one child out of wedlock and doesn't know where the mother and the baby have gone. After another girlfriend became pregnant, he tried to assume responsibility. He moved in with her, and eventually, they decided to marry. But only three months after the baby was born, his wife left him and moved out of state. He followed her and tried to salvage things, but was still unsuccessful. They were both ill-equipped for the responsibilities thrust upon them. The arguments continued, the financial disputes increased, and after 18 months of marriage, they divorced.

I remember his parents very well. They were the cool type mentioned earlier. I met his father only a couple of times; his mother was always around. She was fun, always laughing, and seemed to really love her son. Everyone knew though that Aaron could do whatever he wanted. From his early teens, he bragged about going to the high school parties with his older sister. He would "tell-all" about having sex with his girlfriend nearly every night while both of his parents were home. He installed a lock on his bedroom door, and his parents never bothered to check on them. This was happening during our sophomore year. Is it any surprise that he's experienced serious and untimely problems since then?

I believe that many members of my generation were short-changed when it comes to the sensitive topics of Love and Sex. Parents just didn't discuss it. So many of my peers ended up paying a high price for their avoidable mistakes. I say "avoidable" because so many of them could have avoided premature sexual situations if they had some thoughtful parental guidance.

A story is told about the owner of a sick little dog who finally decided to take him to the veterinarian. They were shown into the examination room and asked to wait. A few minutes later, the doctor came into the room carrying a large gray cat. There was some initial cat/dog tension as the two laid eyes on each other, but soon they both settled down. The vet asked the pet owner to step aside. His dog sheepishly stood alone on top of the steel examination table. The veterinarian then proceeded to walk very slowly around the entire table. He held the cat under his arm while the cat continued to stare intently at the bewildered, old dog. Occasionally, he would move the cat very close to the dog and sometimes even above him. Cautiously, the animals eyeballed each other.

After completing two full rotations around the table, the vet quietly put the cat in a cage and scribbled notes on his chart. He told the owner to give the dog a prescribed medication, and he would be just fine. The vet left the room abruptly.

This unorthodox procedure disappointed the man. He was shocked when he was given the bill on his way out. "Three hundred and seventy-five dollars! We haven't been here for fifteen minutes! What could possibly cost that much?" he complained. The assistant looked over the bill and quietly explained, "Well, sir, you paid $25 for the visit and $350 for the cat-scan."

I'm afraid that in the critical area of Love and Sex, too many children receive a similar "cat-scan" rather than legitimate examinations and reliable diagnoses.

Nearly every one of my male friends was having sex by the ninth grade. Frequent sex. They joked, laughed, and talked about it all the time. And why not? It was fun, and no one had told them not to have sex or given any reasons why they should wait. By our senior year, I was the only one of my male friends who hadn't had sex. I chose not to despite having girlfriends and opportunities.

At home, I was taught that I'd be much better off if sex were reserved until the right time and place, with the right person, and with a lot more maturity. I believed it. I was taught that I would be better off because I would avoid the emotional impact of premature sexual activity as well as the risks of teenage pregnancy. I believed it. I was taught that at the right time I'd have many years to enjoy sexuality without all of the risks, and I believed it.

Many people I knew hopped from bed to bed like rabbits. In doing so, they lost any appreciation for intimacy and never really learned the true meaning of love. Many of them began to take sex for granted and would become insanely jealous when their lover moved on to the next heartthrob. Someday, this practice may serve to break a marriage or a family, not to mention the myriad of heartaches, risks, and resulting difficulties.

I knew many girls in school became pregnant and faced incredibly agonizing choices: to have an abortion, meet the premature responsibilities of motherhood, or give up a newborn for adoption. Each of these choices forces a young girl into a world of emotional and physical dilemmas that they are nowhere near mature enough to cope with. These decisions are far too severe, traumatic, and life-altering to justify the cause. Lives are forever changed.

According to the National Center for Health Statistics, the number of births to unmarried teens has increased by more than 200% since 1960. When teenage girls have babies, life's odds quickly stack against them. Teenagers are far less likely to receive prenatal care, and their babies are less likely to be born healthy. Many teenage mothers don't finish school. If they marry, the chances of divorce are higher than average for teenage couples.

A survey taken in 1989 and featured in Psychology Today reveals that only 11% of young girls indicate that love is their reason for having premarital sex. The leading reasons? Peer pressure, 42%; followed by pressure from boyfriends, 27%; curiosity, 14%; and sexual gratification, 6%.

Boys also cite peer pressure as the primary reason for sexual activity at 43%, followed by curiosity, 24%; everyone is doing it, 17%; and sexual gratification, 10%. Only 6% of males say love is the reason for having sex.

I find it ironic that only 6% of boys and 11% of girls cite love as their reason for having sex when love is one of the most significant reasons for having sex. It's evident that teens are not mature enough to grasp the correlation between love and sex from their own accounts. The second irony is that only 6% to 10% give sexual gratification as their reason for having sex. Yet, Hollywood, TV, and mass media portray sex before and without marriage as incredibly gratifying and glamorous (sex outside marriage is depicted 8-to-1 in TV and movies). After their innocence is lost, young people and adults find out for themselves that gratification in such situations is not all that it appears to be.

In the May 19, 1997 issue of *US News and World Report*, Jennifer Grossman, 30, of MSNBC-TV said, "This all-you-can-eat sexual buffet is leaving a lot of men and women feeling very empty. I see a pattern among all of my girlfriends," she says, "When they sleep with men, they cry. Sleeping with a man you've known for a week is such an 'almost.' It's almost what you want, but a chasm away from what you really need."

Unless learned early on, it may take youth many years of trial and error coupled with failure and disappointment to realize, if they do, that sex is gratifying and beautiful, but under the right conditions. It really can be all they had ever imagined when guarded and expressed with the right person, at the right time, and for the right reason.

For so many young people, there's confusion about the right person, right time, and right reason. Most parents know the answers to these questions but simply neglect to lay down the best law for their kids. For example, who can argue that the parent is not the best one to teach the details of sex, sexuality, why it's beautiful, and why it has its necessary limits? Despite what the parent may have done in the past, who can deny that their child is better off postponing sexual relations? How much risk and emotional confusion can be avoided? Who believes a 12-, 13-, or 14-year-old girl should be allowed to go on one-on-one dates with 16-, 17-, or 18-year-old boys? Why should they? What benefits of such dating outweigh the risks for an easily flattered, naive, and eager-to-please young girl? Why should a 16-, 17-, or 18-year-old boy be allowed to spend every waking moment with a girlfriend? Why should either be allowed out until 1:00 am, somewhere unsupervised or on your couch, for that matter?

I believe the answers to such questions are obvious. Yet, too many parents neglect to set up and enforce necessary guidelines because they think it's unreasonable, impossible, or embarrassing.

This neglect must stop so that we may raise a more successful generation. In the same article from *US News and World Report*, James McHugh, the Catholic bishop of Camden, N.J. points out, "Many young adults who have engaged in sex before marriage aren't so sure they want their younger brothers and sisters to live through the same experience. But they feel restrained from honestly saying what they think to the next generation, either from guilt, ineptitude, or fear that they will be rejected or ridiculed. If everybody's doing it, and everybody accepts that everybody's doing it, then the young man or woman who has a more ennobling vision of human sexuality ends up looking like the oddball."

David Whitman, author of the article, *Pre-Marital Sex: Is It Good for Us?* writes, "...it is hard for parents to, say, convince a 17-year-old that she should abstain from sex now but that when she turns 18 or 21 it will be ok for her to start sleeping with her boyfriends." I can assure you that such an approach just won't work. There must be a clear line of total abstinence drawn in the sand if one hopes to help children avoid the pitfalls of early sexual activity. Even if it means they, and you might be classified as oddballs, I can tell you that I didn't care if I seemed like an oddball or not—I knew that I wasn't.

A friend told me about a girlfriend he had in high school. She couldn't understand why he wouldn't have sex with her at the time. In frustration, she finally sneaked off and had sex with someone who would. They subsequently broke up, and she was pregnant within a year. He now says with a sigh, "I'm certainly glad that wasn't my doing!"

AC Green of the Los Angeles Lakers doesn't mind being an oddball either. At 33 years of age, this basketball star, with the Dallas Mavericks, has yet to find Mrs. Right. What does that mean for AC? "I am still a virgin. Abstaining from extramarital sex is one of the most unpopular things a person can do, much less talk about. From a sheer numbers standpoint, it can be a lonely cause, but that doesn't mean it's not right." He continues, "I abstain as an adult for the same reasons I did as a teen, the principle doesn't change or the feeling of self-respect I get."

Counterintuitively, it seems that there's safety and even strength in being an "oddball." This little story illustrates the point:

Each summer, the Smith family would visit their favorite lake, tucked deep in a forest. Every year as they made the short hike through the woods, they were elated to come over the final ridge and see the funny old tree that stood off on its own, apart from the rest of the forest. It was large and beautiful. It was peculiar, though, because it seemed to twist and bend upward as if it had withstood all of nature's elements. More importantly, this tree indicated to the family that they were just minutes from the final descent leading to the lake.

One year, just a week away from the annual trip, a forest fire scourged the area and destroyed thousands of acres of vegetation. Disappointed but unwilling to break with family tradition, the Smiths decided to keep to their vacation plans. While making the hike through the woods this time, the family was quite somber and in awe of the aftermath. Where beautiful, towering pines once stood there were now blackened and charred trunks. They were saddened at the sight.

As they came over the final ridge, the father glanced back at his family with a great smile. He pointed ahead to the funny old tree. The tree had again stood its ground! Not a leaf had fallen from the branches; its unusual distance had protected it from the rest of the forest. This peculiar old tree was unable to be reached by the consuming flames, and the Smith family delighted in its survival. Its original beauty was now more significant and appreciated than ever before.

Why not arm your children with the best possible defense in a society laden with so many life-altering risks directly related to the abuse of sexuality? Help them stand apart from the crowd. Allow them to be viewed as an oddball if that's what it takes. Allow them to weather the storms of going against popular opinion; it will strengthen them. In the long run, they will develop great personal strength, and they will one day find great satisfaction, maturity, and security in their sexuality.

If you know what's best for them, don't they deserve a Fair Warning concerning this? If they choose to go against your instruction, so be it. You will know that you did everything in your power to lead them along safely. And one day, they will come to appreciate what you have done for them, even if they fight you tooth and nail along the way.

This point reminds me of a parable in William Bennett's *The Book of Virtues*, entitled, *The King and His Hawk* about the great and much-feared warrior, Genghis Khan. One evening, while returning from a day of hunting with his friends, he decided to take a longer route home:

On the king's wrist sat his favorite hawk, for in those days hawks were trained to hunt. At a word from their masters, they would fly high up into the air and look around for prey. If they chanced to see a deer or a rabbit, they would swoop down upon it as swift as any arrow.

Toward evening, they started for home. The king had often ridden through the woods, and he knew all of the paths. So while the rest of the party took the nearest way, he went by a longer road through a valley between two mountains.

The day had been warm, and the king was very thirsty. His pet hawk had left his wrist and flown away. It would be sure to find its way home.

The king rode slowly along. He had once seen a spring of clear water near this pathway. If he could only find it now! But the hot days of summer had dried up all the mountain brooks.

At last, to his joy, he saw some water trickling down over the edge of a rock. He knew that there was a spring farther up. In the wet season, a swift stream of water always poured down here; but now it came only one drop at a time.

The king leapt from his horse. He took a little silver cup from his hunting bag. He held it so as to catch the slowly falling drops. It took a long time to fill the cup; and the king was so thirsty that he could hardly wait. At last it was nearly full. He put the cup to his lips and was about to drink.

All at once there was a whirring sound in the air, and the cup was knocked from his hands. The water was spilled upon the ground.

The king looked up to see who had done this thing. It was his pet hawk.

The hawk flew back and forth a few times, and then alighted among the rocks by the spring.

The king picked up the cup, and again held it to catch the trickling drops. This time, he did not wait so long. When the cup was half full, he lifted it toward his mouth; but before it had touched his lips, the hawk swooped down again, and knocked it from his hands.

And now the king began to grow angry. He tried again, and for the third time, the hawk kept him from drinking. The king was now very angry indeed. "How could you dare to act so?" he cried. "If I had you in my hands, I would wring your neck!"

Then, he filled the cup again. But before he tried to drink, he drew his sword. "Now, Sir Hawk," he said, "this is the last time." He had hardly spoken before the hawk swooped down and knocked the cup from his hand. But the king was looking for this. With a quick sweep of the sword he struck the bird as it passed.

The next moment the poor hawk lie bleeding and dying at its master's feet. "That is what you get for your pains," said Genghis Khan.

But when he looked for his cup, he found it had fallen between two rocks where he could not reach it.

"At any rate, I will have a drink from that spring," he said to himself.

With that he began to climb the steep bank to the place from which the water trickled. It was hard work, and the higher he climbed, the thirstier he became.

At last he reached the place. There indeed was a pool of water; but what was that lying in the pool and almost filling it? It was a huge, dead snake of the most poisonous kind.

The king stopped. He forgot his thirst, he thought only of the poor dead bird lying on the ground below him.

"The hawk saved my life!" he cried, "and how did I repay him? He was my best friend, and I have killed him."

(The King and His Hawk, as retold in The Book of Virtues [Simon & Schuster, New York, 1993], pp. 37–39.)

I will be forever grateful to my parents, my big brothers, and youth leaders who continually knocked the cup of danger from my hands. I didn't see the entire picture initially, and my brothers and I swiped at them with our swords from time to time. In the end, though, each one of us agrees that every rule they attempted to enforce on our behalf in this sensitive area of sexuality, was for our lifelong good.

Children simply are not born able to tell the difference between love and sex. Left unexplained and without rules, great dangers lie in wait for them. I hope that together we can reverse the sentiment held by many and expressed by Neal A. Maxwell when he points out, "Many regard family erosion as regrettable, but not reversible." He further states, "Many who are worried about the spilling of social consequences are busy placing sandbags downstream, while this flooding will yet leave a terrible aftermath in our family gardens."

I believe that the social problems generated by the misuse and lack of regard for love and sex can be reversed. It won't happen by handing out millions of condoms. It won't happen by school districts teaching third graders about every form of sexual activity.

It takes one generation of consistent and unwavering parenting. Take special care of your family garden by building a strong foundation and secure fences, and let others work in vain with temporary sandbag solutions. My generation has endured enough of that!

Parents shouldn't take a lazy approach by telling children that sex is bad or naughty or "just for grown-ups." Such talk only piques interest. Instead, tell them that it's wonderful. Tell them that it's beautiful, exciting, and gratifying. Tell them that they will have many, many years to enjoy it. But tell them that it's so important that life is created by it, and we are brought closer because of it. Tell them that it's best expressed at a time and place where virtually every risk can be eliminated.

Tell them that it's worth the wait!

CHAPTER 11:
Live Your Religion

Whatever may be conceded to the influence of refined education on minds of peculiar structure, reason and experience both forbid us to expect that national morality can prevail in exclusion of religious principle.
—*George Washington, 1796*

Two executives sat and discussed a variety of topics one evening over cocktails. Finally, their discussion swerved into the subject of religion. They began to debate different philosophies cordially.

In frustration, one of the men decided to challenge his friend's merits and taunted, "Darren, don't you try and tell me about religion!" With confidence he continued, "Why, I've got a crisp one-hundred-dollar bill that says you can't even quote the *Ten Commandments*."

"Ha!" Darren responded, "You can kiss that money good-bye!" Totally assured, he took a deep breath, gathered his thoughts, and began, "Our Father, who art in Heaven, hallowed be thy name. Thy Kingdom come, thy will be done; on earth as it is in Heaven. Give us this...." He continued quoting *The Lord's Prayer* verbatim.

The friend who had thrown out the challenge just smiled and shook his head. Then, he handed him the money and said dejectedly, "I'm shocked, Darren. I just didn't think you could do it." Neither man knew the topic, yet both thought they did.

Many people talk the talk when it comes to religion. When it comes to doctrinal knowledge and daily living, though, very few walk the walk. In some cases, they wouldn't even know where to walk if they wanted to. In his book Slouching Towards Gomorrah, Robert Bork says, "It is increasingly clear that very few people who claim religion could truthfully say that it informs their attitudes and significantly affects their behavior."

Religion is much more than a mere professing of belief. Religion is a way of life. It's a set of core spiritual guidelines. It's a contractual agreement one willingly makes with God. It requires sacrifice. It's a standard of living.

Recently, on the *Dr. Laura Schlessinger Show*, a caller complained, "My wife is under the impression that I am not a Christian, but I am!" Dr. Laura explained to him that if his wife had such an impression, she was probably right.

Why this response? Because religion is evident in daily living. It's inherent and becomes apparent in one's day-to-day demeanor. Spend a few days with a devoted Jew, Hindu, Muslim, or Christian, and they will not need to tell you they are religious. You will know they are. You will find out through their speech, actions, and practices. It will naturally surface.

Just this week, I gave a speech in Hollywood, CA. My message centered on the *Fair Warnings* outlined in this book. Because of time constraints, I was unable to address the topic *Live Your Religion*. After my talk, two people came up and asked me if I belonged to a particular Christian sect. I answered that I did, and they said, "We thought so. We could just tell."

I never so much as uttered the word religion in my talk. I never made any reference to my religious affiliation, yet some of them (who, as it turns out, were not members of my faith) surmised my affiliation within 30 minutes. For those who practice their religion, it's visible to others.

This chapter is intended to encourage people to review and reconsider their religious beliefs and their adherence to them. The honest religions of the world exist for the sole purpose of making people and nations better. Who among us cannot benefit from such assistance?

Religions are meant to provide a place of regular worship where one reaffirms their belief in a higher power, renews sacred covenants, improves behavior, gains knowledge, and develops spirituality. Religions offer a core set of principles to which one may wholeheartedly devote him/herself.

Religion is the cement that can hold a person together spiritually and organizationally. It solidifies and validates one's resolve to live according to established guidelines. Religious practice provides many valuable symbols that continuously remind us of our commitments. It makes us accountable and responsible for everything we do. Thus, we're motivated to do everything a little bit better.

Today, there are millions of Jews, Buddhists, Catholics, Protestants, and other members of the many sects of religions. Among those members, many may profess but do not practice their faith. The National Council of Churches reported in 1990 that while there are 148.1 million individuals who claim a religious affiliation, only 28.1 million attend a place of worship regularly or consider themselves practicing. It's disappointing that so few people attend church compared to how many Americans claim to have religious beliefs.

A *TIMES/CNN* poll administered by Yankelovich Partners, Inc. and published in 1997 reported these results when adult Americans were asked the following:

Do you believe in the existence of heaven, where people live forever with God after they die?
81%..........Yes
13%..........No

Do you believe in hell, where people are punished after they die?
63%..........Yes
30%..........No

Do people get into heaven based mostly on the good things they do or on their faith in God or both?
Good things they do..........6%
Faith in God..........34%
Both..........57%

Do you think of heaven as something that is "up there?"
67%..........Yes
29%..........No

Immediately after death, which of the following do you think will happen to you?
Go directly to heaven..........61%
Go to purgatory..........15%
Go to hell..........1%
Be reincarnated..........5%
End of existence..........4%

Is heaven a perfect version of the life we know on earth, or is it totally different?
Perfect version..........11%
Totally different..........85%

Do you believe you will meet friends and family members in heaven when you die?
88%..........Yes
5%.............No

By outlining a few of the things that religion is not, I think we will find out why there are so many believers who are not faithful followers:

1. Religion is not convenient.
2. Religion does not conform socially.
3. Religion takes time.
4. Religion takes money.
5. Religion requires sacrifice.
6. Religion is controversial.
7. Religion puts the responsibility on you.

8. Religion has strict rules.
9. Religion is a daily effort.
10. Religion requires faith.

In short, religion comes with a price fewer and fewer people are willing to pay. People tend to focus on what is not allowed rather than the advantages.

In September 1996, *US News and World Report* indicated that the divorce rate for regular churchgoers is 18%; for those who attend services less than once a year, 34 %. Frequent churchgoers are about 50% less likely to report psychological problems, and 71% are less likely to be alcoholics. The two most reliable predictors of teenage drug avoidance were optimism and regular church attendance.

Religious activity teaches us the tremendous benefits of service. Within a religious community, there are countless opportunities to serve and be served.

While attending law school, my good friend Jim and his wife Suzy were raising two young children. Their youngest, Michael, was diagnosed with cancer. Aside from the difficulties of the situation, as Jim puts it, they didn't have "two nickels to rub together, and dessert consisted of smelling the inside of empty soup cans!" Concerned for their little one and uncertain of his fate, while bound by college and work demands, this young family faced a most difficult crisis.

At the time, Jim and Suzy belonged to a young church congregation of college students. These students shared the same financial status as they did. But they were determined to help in some way. The group decided to put together a fund to help offset the staggering medical costs faced by this family. Everyone in the congregation donated whatever funds they could spare.

The students finally presented the fund. Jim and Suzy opened the meager envelope and carefully counted out $191. It was all the money these people had to give. Yet, they gave. Jim told me that he counts this experience as one of the greatest acts of service their family ever received. They were touched deeply by this singular, humble act. Michael, subsequently healed of his cancer, will teach his children about the $191 gift one day.

My personal experience with religious activity has been transformational. It's the fundamental ingredient holding together all of the Fair Warnings, which my parents shared with me. It enhances my confidence and optimism. It helps me remain focused on the things that matter most.

Religion brings a more unified understanding and communication to a marriage. It helps parents raise their children more effectively and with clear guidelines. It helps family members avoid self-centeredness. It gives parents continuous opportunities to teach their children by example. When integrated and exercised, true religious principles help ordinary people steadily improve in all that they do.

I have virtually no basketball skills. I'm only 5'9", and I can't dribble to save my life. However, allow me to double-dribble, travel, charge, reach, and hack; then, I'll put up a decent challenge.

At a recent family gathering, I played outside myself. I was on fire! Not to mention that I was playing against my nephews, who happen to be far more athletic and physically gifted than I. Rebounding, driving the lane, spinning, hitting shots from everywhere, and blocking, yes, blocking shots. It felt incredible! I hesitate to tell you, for fear of disbelief, but I was dunking for the first time in my life! I should add that my nephews are 8, 10, and 11 years old, respectively, but I assure you that they are quite competitive! And yes, the rim had been lowered to 8', but still.

The beauty of the imagination! And oh, how nice it would be if we could lower the rim of life from time to time. But we can't. There are no shortcuts in life. For every worthy goal each of us seeks, whether it be weight loss, an educational degree, a promotion, a better relationship, breaking a habit, or raising great kids; we reap the rewards only after paying the price.

To gain what religion has to offer, the price is living it. I will never forget a witty and true saying from the pulpit years ago: "Going to church makes you no more of a Christian than sleeping in the garage makes you a Chevrolet!" It only works for us when we put it to work.

So, what's your religion? Do you know and understand what your church teaches? Do you attend? Do you study? Do you believe it? Does it teach principles that you feel in your heart are right and true?

Answer these questions and evaluate your situation. If you're not sure about the teachings of your religion or don't have one, consider setting aside the time to figure it out. Seek out a Faith, ask friends, visit churches, learn to pray. I'm confident that everyone can find the truth and make it a fundamental part of their lives and families.

It's true that for many people, organized religion scares them off. That's understandable. But I believe that if diligent, persistent, and sincere, you can see through the scam operations and inconsistencies. And if you already profess to belong, then help yourself and your family by being true to your beliefs. Study it, live it, and don't just go through the motions. You will then become a master teacher to your children because you teach by example.

In her book *Enjoy the Journey!* Lucile Johnson relates the story of a son's appreciation for his father's ability to teach by example. While giving a talk on Sunday at their church, the young man began, "I was fourteen years old, it was 2:00 a.m., and the TV was on. A terrible storm with thunder had awakened me, and I went down to the TV room. Dad was holding my baby brother and rocking him as he watched. The room was dark except for the light from the TV. I stood in the hall looking in. Dad couldn't see me. Soon, a picture flashed on the screen that was so gross I couldn't believe it! It was really bad! I waited to see what my dad would do. He immediately walked over to the TV and turned it off.

"Dad, I've never told you this, but it really was important to me at that time in my life to see what you would do when no one was looking. I want to say thanks, Dad, thanks for doing what was right." Lucile Johnson was there that day and added, "I watched the father's face as he sat there. He looked stunned and then buried his face in his hands. I felt I knew what was going on in his mind. Later, this father, Evan Bybee told me, 'I can recall that incident vividly. Not knowing my son was standing in the darkness watching, I received a swift and forceful prompting. It said: 'Turn it off.'"

This good father was spiritually in tune. He was then more able to live as he taught his children to live. This opportunity to teach through his example was far more valuable to his son than many years of the spoken word.

Edgar Guest expressed it well with these words:

The eye's a better pupil and more willing than the ear;
Fine counsel is confusing, but examples always clear;
And the best of all the preachers are the men who live their creeds.
For to see the good in action is what everybody needs.
I can soon learn how to do it if you'll let me see it done.
I can watch your hands in action, but your tongue too fast may run;
And the lectures you deliver may be very wise and true,
But I'd rather get my lesson by observing what you do.
For I may misunderstand you and the high advice you give,
But there's no misunderstanding how you act and how you live.

There were a handful of kids I remember, who really stood out among hundreds of high school acquaintances. They were fun, smart, and friendly, but they also had excellent leadership skills. Seemingly beyond their years, they were honorable and complementary to others. Usually, they were not part of the popular party crowd, yet they were very sure of themselves and popular in their own right.

Nearly all of them shared something in common; they came from religious backgrounds. They owned their faith and weren't forced to believe. They had a spiritual family structure that they chose to follow, and it was evident.

There are many teachers, Bishops, Priests, Pastors, and Rabbis who oversee various religious organizations throughout the world. These people assist parents in their objective to raise children to their fullest potential. Isn't it true that everyone relies on another when they can't get along with their parents? In serious matters, your child can turn to a trusted spiritual leader who shares your values, rather than defaulting to one of their inexperienced friends.

My brothers and I would occasionally rebel against regular church attendance and test my parents' ability to make it a regular part of our lives. In the end, our rebellion was not successful. With time and comprehension, we no longer wanted to rebel. Now it has become the foundation of our entire growing family.

This year at church, we had our annual Mother's Day program. A 14-year-old boy named Christian gave a short talk in tribute to his mother. He summed up his message with words, "I am thankful for my mom. Even when I don't want her direction, I am thankful that she gives it."

The myriad of benefits from a religious life is a *Fair Warning* that all children deserve to receive. The rapid decrease in church attendance over the years, as indicated by recent statistics, suggests that many of my generation were brought up without any religion at all. For most of them, it just wasn't part of the plan. Today, many of the Generation Xers I know are uncertain and skeptical about religion. David Briggs, in a recent article featured in *The Salt Lake Tribune* about Generation X and religion, states, "There is less denominational loyalty among Generation

X. Only 31% of [them] report being strongly committed to their denomination...." It will be a shame if their children grow up without the benefits of a religious family structure.

Your children will make the final choice to accept or reject what they learn in the home. Some of them will reject it, and we will still love them unconditionally. But let's not let them leave home without having had every opportunity to develop a spiritual foundation and become the best people they can. Let's not ignore the opportunities we have as parents to become better ourselves. Let's not neglect what it means to our children when we Live Our Religion.

Tell me what you think so far!
Send me a direct message on Instagram:

@_fairwarning_
@jeffchavez_

If you're enjoying this book and know
others who would enjoy it as well, tell them
about <u>Fair Warning</u> on social media, or
pick up a copy for them (now available at
Amazon or Barnes and Noble)!

SECTION FOUR:
A Firm Resolve

CHAPTER 12:
It Can Be Done

There is no chance, no fate, no destiny, that can circumvent or hinder or control the firm resolve of a determined soul.
—Ella Wheeler Wilcox

Lenore Kimbal Nitsch was known to my friend Kris as Aunt Norie. Aunt Norie was unique and inspiration to everyone who knew her. In her own words, she tells of her birth and says, "My wonderful adventure in life began in October 1918. I am sure my arrival did not bring the complete joy my parents anticipated because although my delivery was normal, I was not. Nature had cheated me in not completing her work, and as a result, I came into life with a few permanent physical handicaps. I had Spina Bifida. The malformation was extremely critical, and my life span was expected to be only two weeks. Thus, commenced my sojourn on earth."

Aunt Norie's niece, Kris Pingree, tells her story, "Despite her physical handicap, she had an incredible life. At the age of 21, she finally convinced the board of education to let her go to high school. By this time, they were more concerned about her age than her handicap. But she got to go and finally earned her degree. She went on to marry 'her Siegfried' despite heavy, heavy criticism. She did everything everyone told her she could never do. First, she crawled, then she walked, she read, she went to school, she married, she tended to a garden, she kayaked, she swam, she drove a car, and she lived. But she did not only live, she absolutely, positively thrived.

"At 40, she decided that there was no reason she couldn't learn to kayak. After all, you use your arms, not your legs. So, after a little practice and some lessons, she traveled to Canada to attempt the Bow River. She had her friends and family drop her off at one point, and they agreed to meet a few miles downriver by the highway.

"Norie set off for what was to be about an hour's worth of white-water kayaking. But she came to a fork in the river and chose the wrong way. The left fork took her off course and into a series of rapids that threw her about mercilessly."

Norie recorded, "Things began to happen so fast now that I cannot recall what came first. I do not know how it was, as if with the speed of lightning, that I missed the tree and hit the whirlpool dead center. The boat was immediately sucked from beneath me. The next thing I knew, I was hanging from a huge fallen tree with water dashing around and over me. How my arms got around that great tree, I do not know except the Lord must have been with me."

Kris continues, "Norie managed with just the strength of her arms to shimmy across the tree and to dry ground. She knew she couldn't stay there long but didn't know what to do because her crutches had been lost with the boat. She crawled a little way and happened upon a board that was just an inch shorter than her crutches. With this as her crutch, she began what was to become a two-day ordeal.

"Meanwhile, her friends had notified the authorities that she was missing. They were informed in no uncertain terms that the search would be for the body because there was no way an able person, let alone 'a cripple,' could survive bog country.

"Bog country is a term used for that Canadian wilderness, which consists of brush and undergrowth so thick it's virtually impossible to move through. It also includes dense swamp areas, which means millions of mosquitoes. Sometimes, the muck in the swamp was so thick, Norie would literally get stuck in it and spend hours working herself loose. In addition to all that, temperatures at night dropped well below freezing, and it was in bear country.

"For two days, she crawled through this brush, shimmied across a dozen trees to avoid the swamps, and slept under a tree praying that she wouldn't happen upon a bear. After forty-eight hours, she finally was in sight of the highway. She crawled up an extremely steep embankment to the highway, sat by its side, and waited. But by then, the search had been called off, and friends and family had been notified of her death. The hours passed, and finally, someone drove by, and she was rescued.

"It turns out that up until that point in history, Norie was the only person to have ever survived being dumped into the Bow River. And it turns out there had been many an adventurer who had tried. Every Park Ranger in the area had given her up for dead. But when they heard of her survival, every one of them came to meet 'the cripple' who had crawled through Bog Country."

I would love to have met Aunt Norie, too. She truly "made it" in life, and she did it despite the odds stacked heavily against her. She decided early on to excel and systematically went forward to attain that goal. Even life-threatening setbacks and obstacles were, to her, only temporary delays.

Some parents today aren't even attempting to enforce standards. The odds seem to be too heavily stacked against their children. I have heard people scoff at the notion of asking a teenager to abstain from sex. "It's an impossible expectation!" they retort. I have heard people insist, "Everyone has to party a little in life!" And many doubt that a parent can be a child's closest friend, "He'll just do what his friends want before he'll do something for me," they say. And today, many feel that "If I can just get her to graduate from high school, I'll be happy."

These are limiting thoughts. There are millions of kids who would develop lives free from the dangers we've discussed if given clear-cut rules and then taught how and why they should adhere to them. I happen to personally know of hundreds of Generation Xers who lived with such guidance, accepted it, and are succeeding far beyond what is reported by the media.

Some of them live just as they were shown and taught by their parent or parents. Some of them rebelled, slipped-up, or faltered along the way, and many of them may continue to do so. But all have a clear path they can choose to follow, and most of them are doing that. Why? Because it makes sense. They see and have experienced the benefits. Now they can teach their children how to walk that higher road as well.

James Allen once said, "He who cherishes a beautiful vision, a lofty ideal in his heart will one day realize it." I encourage parents to believe, regardless of their past experiences and weaknesses, that their family can rise above the negative national statistics and begin a family legacy of moral, spiritual, and personal greatness. And I'm confident that our entire nation will be the better for it within a generation or two.

In my short life, I've learned that we need two things to succeed in our quest for success. One is a clear vision of where we're going, and the second is a plan to get there.

I don't know how many times I've been shown how to do something correctly yet tried to do it in my own, unproven way. I've had to pay the price for these mistakes many times over the years.

One of these mistakes took place on a surfing trip to Pismo Beach nearly ten years ago. I was excited to surf a new area, and my friends took me out the first day to a beach with cliffs and a very rocky coastline.

To make it out to this little reef break about 1/4 mile offshore, we had to hike down a rocky trail. I followed their every footstep while traversing the steep terrain. I could see the danger if I didn't follow every step. They knew what they were doing, and we made it to the water safely.

We stood on some rocks that were in a cove protected from the oncoming surf. They explained the course we were to take, and I agreed to paddle just as they had shown me. Our designated path was to paddle in the opposite direction of the actual surf spot. First, we had to paddle around a large rock and then to where the waves were breaking on the reef.

My friends both jumped into the water and quickly paddled away. I was hesitant to follow them because the route they were taking was more than double the distance that seemed necessary. I could see I could cut the distance in half by paddling straight towards the reef rather than out and around the big rock.

The water was smooth, and there was no visible activity out on the reef. I knew what I was doing, so I jumped on my board and paddled straight ahead. I was sure to catch a couple of waves for myself before my friends got there.

At first, I was delighted with my decision and began to chuckle to myself, wondering why they took the long route. With a third of the way to go, I noticed some waves starting to rise on the reef. The surf was about four feet that day, creating wave faces of six to eight feet in height. I wasn't worried, though, because it was a simple task to duck dive under the oncoming waves. As I neared the reef and prepared to dive under the first wave, my hand hit a sharp rock under me. Suddenly, I realized that I was in less than two feet of water! Unbeknownst to me, there was an inside reef, which was much shallower and exposed than the actual surf break, and here I was directly over that reef. It would be impossible to duck dive under the oncoming waves!

Frantically, I threw my board to the side and held on to a submerged rock. I managed to hold on as the first wave passed. As a second, larger wave approached though, it pulled the remaining water from the reef as it gained speed and strength. I was standing in less than a foot of water as this eight-foot wall of ocean came toward me, and I was being sucked toward it! All I could do was dive straight into it just as the lip of the wave was pitching outward. I didn't make it through the wave and was sucked back over the falls, and was pummeled onto the now nearly exposed rock pile. The next wave tossed me across the shallow rocks and eventually pushed me into the deeper water. I slumped over floating on my back, gasping for air.

Luckily, I was wearing a wet suit, which protected me from getting chewed up by the rocks. The two holes on my knees and shoulder ruined the suit for good.

Humiliated, I climbed back onto my surfboard, which now had a shattered fin, and paddled back to our starting point. I paddled out and around the big rock just as we had initially planned. I was happy to be alive! I only wished I had done it the way my friends had told me in the first place.

Once you have set your sights on that lofty vision of what is possible for your family, once you have outlined a clear, proven course, forget the shortcuts; forget how long it may take. Just commit to sticking to that course.

There will be mishaps and setbacks along the way. Sometimes, we'll drop the ball. But remember in those moments, "It doesn't matter if you try and fail, but if you fail, and fail to try again!"

Many families will draft a mission statement or a family constitution. It's meant to clarify beliefs and give structure. It enables families to discuss and consider different ways to implement teachings and beliefs.

A family plan can include a commitment to something as simple as eating dinner together. And what a powerful impact something like this can have. A poll on education by Reader's Digest in 1994 found, "Sixty percent of students who said their 'whole family sits around a table together for a meal' at least four times a week got high scores on a general education quiz, which they distributed. Of students in families that ate together three times a week or less, just 42% scored high, a huge 18-point gap."

Other specific family plans can include setting aside one night each week as pure family time. No extra-curricular activities are scheduled that night: no TV, no telephone calls, just family time. Play games, tell jokes, laugh together, teach principles, learn stuff, and talk about real things.

I can recall the difficulty my parents had with us boys when they initially tried to implement a family night. When they first started it, we were already about 8, 12, and 16 years old. We were not very cooperative. Our first organized family nights seemed more like a family home rumble. Nobody followed instructions, nobody could agree on a game, and mom accidentally burnt the popcorn. Had my parents begun years earlier, it probably would have been more successful. We did hold a family home evening from time to time, more spontaneous than structured, but even that little bit made a difference.

I'm thankful my parents didn't give up when we gave them a hard time and when they might have felt that they were failing.

I remember one night when my dad heard some commotion in the front yard. He went into my brother Greg's room near the balcony at the front of the house. He opened Greg's door and asked, "Hey, what's all that noise in the front yard?" The room was dark, and dad couldn't see in very well. From the darkness, he heard an unfamiliar voice respond, "I think some kids are tee-peeing your house, Mr. Chavez." He ruffled his brow and thought, "Mr. Chavez?!" Dad immediately flipped on the light to find our teenage neighbor Frank, in Greg's bed covering for him while he snuck out for the night.

And Brother Chris had legal action taken against him once when he turned his windshield wiper fluid nozzles outward and sprayed my crossing guard in the eye. He also had an uncanny ability to push every nerve-bending button known to parents. Chris generated more, "I've had-it-up-to-HERE!" proclamations from our mom than any of us.

I learned to push those buttons with precision as well. Like the time mom threw a glass of water in my face when I drove her to the brink. All the mothers of the world would have cheered wildly had they witnessed that scene.

One night, I was dragged from The Camarillo Cinema and escorted home after one of my friends caused near pandemonium in a packed movie theater. He stole a foot-long strand of magnesium from science class and decided to light it in the middle of the movie. Magnesium, when ignited, burns brighter than the sun. The entire theater illuminated as if struck by lightning! The moviegoers were not in the least bit amused, and all of us were promptly ejected.

I expect my kids to pay me back for the antics and frustrations I caused my parents. But whatever happens, I won't shy away from high standards.

As I've said, this book isn't a step-by-step program for familial success. It's a reality check, parent-to-parent. It's a plea to go above and beyond and give your children the best shot at success. I've outlined a few Fair Warnings, which every parent can and should extend to their children.

This will be more difficult for some than for others. Some may have to make many personal changes before they can effectively enforce these guidelines. Some struggling marriages need repair. Some apologies need to be made. Broken trust may need to heal.

Whatever your situation may be, I'm asking you to pay the price. I'm asking you to take inventory of your life and consider your family's state or plans for your future family. I'm asking you to make this country great by making yourself great. I'm asking you to allow your children the opportunity to become better than they might be. I'm asking you to treat yourself to the best life possible by living and extending Fair Warning to your children.

I challenge you to commit to personal and familial progression. We all have room for improvement. We can all do so much more.

You can study the best books on personal improvement or spirituality. Devour books on the family and relationships so that you might create an effective plan. Learn from scriptures or other sacred writings. Seek advice from those you love and admire. Get counseling or additional professional help if you need to. Step outside of yourself and consider what kind of legacy you'll leave for your family and your community.

Why not attempt to live as one of my mentors, Garth Eames has lived? He's a humble potato farmer from Rupert, Idaho. In his later years, he simply stated, "I have no regrets."

More than 90 years old, Gordon B. Hinckley once joked, "My wife and I are finding that these golden years are laced with lead!" Amidst the inevitable, natural difficulties of old age, what a great thing it will be to look back on our lives as Garth Eames did and declare, "I have no regrets!"

British statesman, Edmund Burke, warned, "All that is necessary for the triumph of evil is that good men do nothing." Let us not be complacent. Let us do something worthwhile. You and your children can't afford complacency, and neither can society. The risks are too significant.

Change, even on a national scale, can become a reality. It can be done! It can be done with the wise help from our grandparents and Boomers. It can be done by my own Generation X, who is now entering the season of parenting. And it can be carried on by our children and our children's children!

If we do this, we will not only make our own "...*Good Children Great,*" but also become "...*American Heroes.*"

Afterword, 2020

Now 49 years old, I've gained some life experience. The ups and downs of the last two decades have allowed me to try to apply what I've written. Spoiler alert: It isn't easy! You will fail sometimes!

If you skipped the opening segment of this book, *Twenty-Three Years Later,* please go back and read it. I disclosed how I failed to heed all the *Fair Warnings* that I've presented and the heavy consequences that followed. Through it all, I've learned that what matters most is that we get back up and keep trying, no matter how long and hard the road. Our greatest accomplishments require all that we can possibly give.

Today, I get to watch my kids navigate their young lives, trying to apply the principles—trying to heed the Fair Warnings that their parents worked hard to pass along to them. So far, it's going well. Not perfect. Lots of mistakes are happening to be sure—but these kids are getting back up and trying again and again. They are becoming great contributors to our social fabric because they keep trying to get better and improve. Nothing makes me happier. Nothing gives me more hope for their future.

To be sure, my transparency proves that I'm not the ideal parent to model. I'm the passionate messenger in this story. I believe wholeheartedly in the message. Along my journey in family leadership, I've learned so much from watching and observing others. We have many examples from whom to learn. If we pay attention, we'll see them all around us, we'll improve because of their example. They might be within our extended families, living in our neighborhoods, or sitting across from us at a restaurant. As we conclude, permit me to share one of my favorite examples of family leadership from recent American history:

In 1954, she was born to John and Angelena in Birmingham, Alabama. These young, black parents wondered how they would successfully guide their daughter through what would undoubtedly be a life of segregation and discrimination. Like generations before her, she would need to adapt and persist despite the odds stacked against her.

Years later, in her memoirs, she describes Birmingham of that era as "eclipsing every other big American city in the ugliness of its racism." Her parents and recent ancestors were well acquainted with discrimination and oppression, "My great-great-grandmother Zina on my mother's side bore five children by different slave owners," and "My great-grandmother on my father's side, Julia Head, carried the name of the slave owner and was so favored by him that he taught her to read." Amid so much darkness, Julia learned to read. It was the faintest of silver linings, but a ray of light nevertheless. By focusing on this small and simple skill, rather than on the negativity of her past, she began to pave the way toward a future of greatness for the next generations.

John was a Presbyterian minister, and her mother, Angelena, a school teacher. Without money or social advantages, they were determined to raise a young woman who would reach her full potential. She says her parents had her convinced "that even if I couldn't have a hamburger at Woolworth's lunch counter, I could grow up to be president of the United States." Their strategy was straightforward. They would create a home that was dedicated to learning, character, responsibility, and faith.

As a girl, she was expected to take on any educational and leadership opportunity that arose. If it would build character and self-discipline, she was encouraged to jump in. "I would even say that my parents, and their friends in our community, thought of education as a kind of armor against racism," she says. "If you were well-educated and you spoke well, then there was only so much 'they' could do to you."

In the modest home of John and Angelena Rice, education, character, and self-discipline, served "…as a kind of armor…" against life's obstacles. Call it armor, call it Fair Warning, these committed parents of a young and impressionable Condoleezza Rice were determined to give her every possible opportunity to thrive in this world.

And thrive she has. Ms. Condoleezza Rice became the first woman and first person of color to serve as provost of Stanford University. In 2001, Rice was appointed national security adviser by President George W. Bush, becoming the first black woman (and woman) to hold the post, and went on to become the first black woman to serve as U.S. Secretary of State. In August 2012, Rice and South Carolina businesswoman Darla Moore became the first women to (simultaneously) become members of the Augusta National Golf Club. The event was monumental: The Augusta National Golf Club, which opened in 1933, had infamously been known for its all-male membership and repeated failure to admit women.

Reflecting on the expectations of her parents, Rice says, "I think my father thought I might be president of the United States. I think he would've been satisfied with secretary of state. I'm a foreign policy person, and to have a chance to serve my country as the nation's chief diplomat at a time of peril and consequence, that was enough."

Without question, her parents must be proud and grateful for the influential woman that she's become. But when asked about her many notable accomplishments, Rice seems more interested in telling the stories of the defining lessons she learned from her parents about how to overcome life's obstacles and injustices. She says, regarding racism in particular that she cherishes, "how my parents, and our community, reacted to it—not being beaten down by it, not even being particularly bitter about it. But rather, believing, 'Well, you may not have been able to control those circumstances, but you could control how you reacted to your circumstances.' Maybe that's a good story for people to know." *(Excerpts from* Extraordinary, Ordinary People: A Memoir of Familiar *by Condoleezza Rice. Copyright 2010 by Condoleezza Rice.)*

170 | *FAIR WARNING*

American familial success stories like the Rices' are indeed good stories that we should know and to which we can aspire. How many young people might have amounted to so much more if their parents, or parent, or guardian, was committed to a straightforward strategy like the Rices? What if hundreds of thousands of American parents of every race and creed would model the example of John and Angelena Rice by creating homes dedicated to learning, character, responsibility, and faith?

Maybe then, this country will look less chaotic, broken, angry, and conflicted, and more as our Founding Fathers and Mothers envisioned: an America that's joyful and united in *Life, Liberty, and the Pursuit of Happiness.*

About The Author

Jeff Chavez is a writer, speaker, and entrepreneur residing in Fallbrook, CA. Between surfing, running, reading, and writing, he and his wife are working hard to raise seven great kids.

To learn more:
www.jeffchavez.net

Instagram:
@_fairwarning_
@jeffchavez_

Twitter:
@jeffchavez